Women Writers

WOMEN IN ROMANTICISM

Mary Wollstonecraft, Dorothy Wordsworth and Mary Shelley

Meena Alexander

BARNES & NOBLE BOOKS
SAVAGE, MARYLAND

First published in the USA 1989 by
BARNES & NOBLE BOOKS
8705 Bollman Place
Savage, Maryland 20763

Printed in Hong Kong

ISBN: 0–389–20884–1 Cloth
      0–389–20885–X Paper

Library of Congress Cataloging in Publication Data
Alexander, Meena, 1951–
Women in romanticism: Mary Wollstonecraft, Dorothy Wordsworth,
and Mary Shelley / Meena Alexander.
p. cm. — (Women writers)
Bibliography: p.
Includes index.
ISBN 0–389–20884–1.   0–389–20885–X (pbk.)
1. English literature—19th century—History and criticism.
2. Romanticism—England.   3. Women and literature—England.
4. English literature—Women authors—History and criticism.
5. Wollstonecraft, Mary, 1759–1797—Criticism and interpretation.
6. Wordsworth, Dorothy, 1771–1855—Criticism and interpretation.
7. Shelley, Mary Wollstonecraft, 1797–1851—Criticism and
interpretation.   I. Title.   II. Series.
PR457.A45   1989
820.9'145—dc20   89–7009
                                                      CIP

WOMEN IN ROMANTICISM

Women Writers

General Editors: *Eva Figes* and *Adele King*

Published titles:

Sylvia Plath, Susan Bassnett
Fanny Burney, Judy Simons
Christina Stead, Diana Brydon
Charlotte Brontë, Pauline Nestor
Margaret Atwood, Barbara Hill Rigney
Eudora Welty, Louise Westling
Anne Brontë, Elizabeth Langland
Women in Romanticism, Meena Alexander

Forthcoming:

Jane Austen, Meenakshi Mukherjee
Elizabeth Barrett Browning, Marjorie Stone
Elizabeth Bowen, Phyllis Lassner
Emily Brontë, Lyn Pykett
Ivy Compton Burnett, Kathy Gentile
Willa Cather, Susie Thomas
Colette, Diana Holmes
Emily Dickinson, Joan Kirkby
George Eliot, Kristin Brady
Mrs Gaskell, Jane Spencer
Doris Lessing, Barbara Hill Rigney
Katherine Mansfield, Diane DeBell
Christina Rossetti, Linda Marshall
Jean Rhys, Carol Rumens
Stevie Smith, Catherine Civello
Muriel Spark, Judith Sproxton
Edith Wharton, Katherine Joslin-Jeske
Virginia Woolf, Clare Hanson

Contents

For David

'Printing in the infernal method, by corrosives, which in Hell are salutary and medicinal, melting apparent surfaces away.'

William Blake

List of Plates

Editors' Preface

The study of women's writing has been long neglected by a male critical establishment both in academic circles and beyond. As a result, many women writers have either been unfairly neglected or have been marginalised in some way, so that their true influence and importance has been ignored. Other women writers have been accepted by male critics and academics, but on terms which seem, to many women readers of this generation, to be false or simplistic. In the past the internal conflicts involved in being a woman in a male-dominated society have been largely ignored by readers of both sexes, and this has affected our reading of women's work. The time has come for a serious reassessment of women's writing in the light of what we understand today.

This series is designed to help in that reassessment.

All the books are written by women because we believe that men's understanding of feminist critique is only, at best, partial. And besides, men have held the floor quite long enough.

EVA FIGES
ADELE KING

Preface

When I first began to read William Wordsworth and Romantic poetry, I was a young child in India. Like many other young children receiving an English education in a post-colonial world, I had to learn his 'Daffodils' poem by heart. I had no idea what the flower looked like. Many years later, with a shock of recognition, I caught sight of those fleshly yellow petals in a Nottingham wood. It was still years later, in North America now, that I read Dorothy Wordsworth. She stunned and delighted me. Little in my education had prepared me for the complex precision of her writing, or its fragmentary and feminine nature. Reading Dorothy, I turned round. I sought out the writings of that passionate woman Wollstonecraft and then the fierce work of her daughter Mary Shelley. I was reeducating myself, learning afresh about Romanticism, glimpsing covert strategies in those who had no power, sensing a more hidden turmoil than in the grand displays one prizes in the male poets. Reading and writing about these three women has brought me closer to home.

I am grateful to friends who have helped me through this project, listening and talking over a cup of coffee, pointing out difficulties, making further suggestions. Some have helped me read hard manuscripts, others have taken care and trouble to read these writings at various stages. To Svati Joshi, Walter Kendrick, Beth Darlington, Joel Porte, James Boulton, Yi-Fu Tuan, John Maynard, Florence Boos, Susan Sherman, Stephen Parrish, Norman Fruman, James Earl, Philip Sicker, Vivian Gornick, Alice Fredman, Martin Roth, Richard Leppert, James McGavran, J. Robert Barth S.J., Paul Betz, Richard Barickman, I send my thanks. My thanks to Adele King and Eva Figes, series editors and to

Vanessa Peerless, Beverley Tarquini and Caroline Egar of Macmillan.

Thanks are due to those who generously helped me at Grasmere: Jonathan Wordsworth, Chairman of the Wordsworth Trust and Terry McCormick, Resident Curator of the Wordsworth Library. I am grateful to The Dove Cottage Trust for permission to study and quote from the Dorothy Wordsworth manuscripts preserved in Grasmere. Thanks to the Berg Collection of the New York Public Library and to Donald Reiman and Mihai Handrea of The Carl H. Pforzheimer Shelley and his Circle Collection of the New York Public Library for access to relevant materials on Mary Wollstonecraft and Mary Shelley. I am grateful to Oxford University Press for permission to quote from the six volume set of *The Letters of William and Dorothy Wordsworth*; Mary Moorman's *Journals of Dorothy Wordsworth*; Ernest de Selincourt's editions of *George and Sarah Green, A Narrative* and *The Poetical Works of William Wordsworth*; Mary E. Burton's edition of *The Letters of Mary Wordsworth*. I am grateful to W.W. Norton for permission to quote from Adrienne Rich's *Dream of a Common Language*. Some of the thoughts on Dorothy Wordsworth were first published in my essay 'Dorothy Wordsworth: The Grounds of Writing' which appeared in *Women's Studies* vol. 14, no. 3 (1988) and I am grateful for permission to reprint portions of it. I have benefited from a Summer Seminar Grant, and a Travel Grant from the NEH (National Endowment for the Humanities), a Grant-in-Aid from the ACLS (American Council of Learned Societies) and a Fordham Faculty Research Grant, each of which helped the work along.

In the course of my writing, my son Adam Kuruvilla grew up and my little daughter Svati Mariam was born. The heart of what I have learnt about maternity, a recurrent theme in this book, comes from them. My husband David

Lelyveld has cared for me and supported my poems and prose writings. I have learnt more from him than I could ever put into words.

Introduction: Mapping a Female Romanticism

Beyond Subservience

A little girl, who is teaching herself to write before she can read, starts with the letter 'O'. 'To begin with, she would write nothing but O's; she was always making O's large and small, of all kinds and one within another, but always drawn backwards.'[1] Suddenly, the little girl stops short and catches a glimpse of herself in the mirror. Discomfited by her appearance, she flings away her pen. After that she refuses to write again. Only the threat of misplacing her clothes induces her to continue. She learns how to write in order to mark them with her name.

This story from *Émile* (1762), Jean Jacques Rousseau's treatise on education, is meant to show that reading and writing, the whole command of the symbolic, can only be a 'fatal knowledge' as far as the little girl is concerned. They intrude on her true tasks, the discrete, practical activities involved in running a household. While teaching herself how to write, the child has stumbled against her own image. As Rousseau makes clear, she could not tolerate 'the look of the thing.' (*E*.332)

Rousseau's tale captures a vision of the feminine that the women writers considered in this book, each in her own way, had to struggle against. He sees the girl – she prefigures the state of the grown woman – forced to stop short in her writing precisely because of her dismay at her appearance as she writes. The way she looks as she writes is unfeminine, and hence 'unnatural'. As Mary Wollstonecraft, Rousseau's first feminist critic realised, this Romantic vision of what

1

was natural to women was a reflection of social constraints. It was not a necessary condition of a woman's life. The idea of femininity had to be radically questioned and exposed for what it was, a man-made notion.

Mary Wollstonecraft was born in 1759. She died in 1797, eleven days after giving birth to an infant girl who grew up to be the writer Mary Shelley. Mary Shelley lived until 1851. Dorothy Wordsworth was born in 1771, a year and a half after her famous brother William whom she outlived by five years. She died in 1855, having spent the last two decades of her life in the darkness of a physical and mental deterioration, the cause of which is not fully known.

A mother and a daughter, a sister and a brother: powerful familial bonds that fuse the separate strands of creativity in the works of three women writers whose lives spanned the era of English Romanticism. It is a difficult passage from Wollstonecraft's revolutionary fervour, her ardent belief in the claims of social justice for all human beings regardless of sex, to the resolutely private world of Dorothy Wordsworth, her genius intimately bound to the complicated, meditative powers of her poet brother. With Mary Shelley, a second generation Romantic, we enter a harsh visionary world. Her female longings are bound to radical loss, failures of compassion, abrupt endings. Through these three women, one may track the growth and decay of Romantic knowledge.

But the map is not of the usual sort. The claims of Romantic subjectivity are questioned, undermined and finally refashioned in these writings. Where the Romantic poets had sought out the clarities of visionary knowledge, women writers, their lives dominated by the bonds of family and the cultural constraints of femininity, altered that knowledge, forcing it to come to terms with the substantial claims of a woman's view of the world. But cutting against the 'minute attention to propriety' or even the grace of feminine images in Romantic poetry was only part of the story.[2] Beneath the embattled surface of women's writing, lay a less obtrusive search: for new forms of literary knowledge, for a territory shaped by the truths of a female life.

To grow up female in the age of Dorothy Wordsworth was to recognise that the world of women was distinct if inseparable from that of men. The inner-outer dichotomy the Romantic poets played with presupposed a centralising self that could not be easily translated into the world of women. Born into a realm of implicit subservience, however privileged its immediate nature, women often grasped the public world as difficult, if not inimical to their aspirations. To state this flat out is not to deny the achievement of women of letters, several of whom earned their living by the pen. Wollstonecraft thought of herself as 'the first of a new genus'. (*WL*.164) She was not alone in her endeavour. Before and after her, women in England not only wrote for a living but became major literary figures. Still the condition of ordinary women's lives cannot be ignored.

Through detailed household tasks, women preserved the fabric of ordinary life. They cared for the young, watched over the sick and dying, supported other women in childbirth. Birth and death, the fragile passages in and out of existence, even if sanctified by the patriarchal authority of Church and family, were held within the world of women. Indeed the persistent difficulties of female creativity in the Romantic era had to do with the struggle to capture a subjectivity that endured and supported the fabric of daily life, haunted always by a sense of subservience.

Built into the self-conscious ponderings of Romantic poetry, the ruminations on sensory perception and spiritual power, were concepts of hierarchy and authority that male poets could take for granted. A pained, questing consciousness in search of ever more elusive truths was upheld by a social code of implicit autonomy, and permission for acts of power. Whether in the fierce prophetic vein of William

Blake, in William Wordsworth's convoluted reckonings with memory, or Percy Shelley's edgy scepticism, the Romantic poets sought a vision that assumed the authority of self-consciousness. That took as a right the intense, seemingly unremitting complications of poetic thought. I am not saying that the heights of poetic meditation were easy to achieve, that doubt and dismay were not woven into the fabric of this knowledge, or that it was a monolithic whole. But when set beside women's writings, the implicit assumption of power in male writing is cast into relief.

The woman writer had to cut through the bonds of femininity, those structures of patriarchal authority that seemed to stand outside her, though powerfully gathered in to her intimate grasp of self, even as she set about the slow and often difficult task of discovering the sources of her own genius. In a gendered world, as Mary Wollstonecraft painfully discovered, knowledge was never unmarked.

But given the powerful male tradition, how were women to face the 'anxiety of authorship'?[3] In the Romantic era one discovers two types of female writing. On the one hand, there is a meditative structure gathering strength from an abnegation of the overt will to power, as in Dorothy Wordsworth's *Alfoxden and Grasmere Journals*, or portions of Wollstonecraft's *Letters from Sweden*. On the other hand is a fierce, even violent confrontation with masculine obsession or male authority as in Wollstonecraft's *Maria* and Mary Shelley's *Frankenstein* and *Mathilda*. Both types are strategies for overcoming the anxiety of feminine inadequacy, playing against it, turning it on its head.

These women writers developed what might be called a back-against-the-wall aesthetic. For the mythic power of personal symbols, so critical to Romantic poetry, they substituted bits and pieces of their own bodily selves. Obviously it is impossible to put into a poem, novel or journal, actual and substantial bits of one's physicality, to stick 'brute reality' as it were into the text. It is possible, however, to get as close as one can to such an activity: draw on the substantial, bodily self, like Dorothy Wordsworth, who kept walking in her journals, or Wollstonecraft's imprisoned Maria, who drew inspiration from her painfully swollen breasts, or Mary Shelley who in fierce, contorting acts of the imagination drew on bits and pieces of dead bodies for a monster that could never be naturally birthed. Each writer in her own way struggled to construct a world that in large measure, and at least for the time of composition, was freed from the brutal demands of subservience.

In their distrust of the canonical forms of literature, women writers turned to the concrete world around them. The aesthetic orders they forged never strayed too far from their origins in daily life or the values of a communal existence. The resolutions available to women writers involved recapturing a life shared with others even if the knowledge was darkened by a despair that could not readily be translated into a metaphysic.

By highlighting the change wrought by the seeing self, the eye/I, the great poets of English Romanticism established a distinctive mode of capturing the real. And the political radicalism that Blake, the young Wordsworth and Shelley shared with many others served to sharpen this absorption in the act of vision. The centrality of the poet's self was crucial to an art that tried to free itself of pre-determined orders, whether literary or political. The world could not be remade without visionary freedom.

For women writers this Romantic ideal of selfhood and its visionary freedom was not easy to come by. Nor did it always seem to be singularly appropriate to women. The Romantic self presupposed a self-consciousness that had the leisure and space to enshrine itself at the heart of things. Brought up with a very different sense of the self, with constant reminders of how their lives were meshed in with other lives in bonds of care and concern, women could not easily aspire to this ideal. Indeed, to some women writers it seemed patently false, or wrong-headed. And just as difficult for women was the Romantic vision of the feminine. It might be gentle, nurturing and silent, or fiercely sexual and fatal; but nowhere was it granted a genius commensurate with that of men.

If the essence of Romantic art lies in the keen emphasis on subjectivity, a fascination with the activities of the poet's imagination as it remakes the visible world, women writers standing where they did in the shared world questioned that intense self-absorption. They turned their literary powers to a clarification of genius that had to struggle through its enforced marginality, work against images that would deplete it of power. The freedom, solitary and boundless, sometimes seen in Romantic writing, however exhilarating it might be, had little place in the work of women. If anything it forced women writers to a careful scrutiny of their own lives.

Male Romantics frequently valued the concrete image, the particle of the physical world that could be turned into symbol. Concretion provided a vivid, incontrovertible starting point for a mind enamoured of the visionary. Blake, uncomfortable though he was with Wordsworthian naturalism had set the concrete particular at the heart of his poetics. A grain of sand might disclose a whole world; heaven might be glimpsed in a wild flower. Wordsworth for his part was resolute in attacking all those who might veer towards abstractions, even his dear friend Coleridge. In *The Prelude* we read his somewhat pained critique of Coleridge whose eloquence and learning seemed to the poet a 'wild ideal pageantry', mere words lacking a hold of the substantial world. Coleridge's poems seemed to Wordsworth to be 'shaped out':

From things well-matched, or ill, and words for things –
The self-created sustenance of a mind

Debarred from Nature's living images,
Compelled to be a life unto itself . . . [4]

Picturing his friend as this glorious frenetic mind,
Wordsworth could subtly highlight what he viewed as
his own adherence to the natural world and the solid
truths it afforded the poet. But nature was of course only
a starting point for Wordsworth. His true material lay in
reflections on how the imagination worked, the very act of
making meaning, the 'picture of the mind' as he called it
in 'Tintern Abbey'. There is a contrast here with his sister
Dorothy's work. In her writings, the natural world, in all
its delicate detail stands as the end point of vision. The
boundaries of the visible are illumined in her work. She
remains within them and within the shared world. Seen
from the perspective of her writings, her brother's work, in
all its grandeur, edged by an imagined metaphysics, seems
isolated, apart. His genius might even justify the use of the
phrase he applied to Coleridge, a mind 'compelled to be a
life unto itself'.

The belief in individual subjectivity that led to the
Romantic fascination with the processes of imagination, also
nourished a political radicalism. Searching out marks of the
mind's activity was compatible with a belief in revolution,
a desire to overthrow oppressive social orders. The French
and American revolutions gave actuality to Romantic belief.
At times the New World seemed very close at hand, a fresh
order created through human energies.

Cut free of the stamp of an earlier classicism, Romantic
poetry bears within itself inklings of the processes of mind
that brought it into being. By the same token it offers
glimpses of its own unravelling, a sense of the provisional
nature of all order, a sense of a greater hidden chaos. This
implicit power of decreation might be considered ironic, a
mode of Romantic irony, ultimately 'a way of keeping in
contact with a greater power'.[5]

For women in Romanticism the play of possibility was rather different. Those who were inspired by the political struggles in France and America, or closer at hand in England, drew strength from an art that had no real counterpart in male writing. Women writers had to resurrect and heal a self that was mutilated by the societal vision of what was permitted a woman. In dealing with the chaos inflicted by society the woman writer glimpsed a power within her own psyche. Its order and disorders were ultimately free, beyond societal manipulation. Turning to the origins of her power the woman writer had to face the strictures of society. Yet she could reclaim a knowledge that male Romanticism could not touch, the experience of her own body. Turning to what lay closest most intimately to hand, women in Romanticism forged an art that undercut the presumptions of power in the great poetry of the age. The knowledge of maternity and the nurture of the young lay closely entwined in this bodily knowledge.

'Tangled in a Woman's Body'

In a well known passage Virginia Woolf conjures up the hypothetical fate of a gifted young woman, Judith Shakespeare, born to the same parents as the great playwright. How would she have lived her life? What would she have written? Woolf imagines her poverty, her lack of any opportunity to study, read or write. Judith hides out in the apple loft, she scribbles a few pages, she runs off to London, she falls into sex, she becomes pregnant. Despair and shame consume her. The end is evident. She kills herself. 'Who shall measure the heat and violence of the poet's heart when caught and tangled in a woman's body?'[6]

William Wordsworth, the great poet of English Romanticism, did have a sister, Dorothy, to whom he was deeply attached. From time to time he speaks of her in his poetry. Often in his earlier years he mined her *Alfoxden* (1798) and *Grasmere Journals* (1800-3), a rich source of their shared, communal knowledge, for precise images and refined reflections for his own poems. Dorothy was a copious writer: a storm of letters, journals, travelogues, poems and two narratives. All her adult life she lived with her brother, helping keep house, sharing his literary reflections, the ups and downs of his creativity, the demands of his growing family.

She also, quite consciously, made the decision not to publish, not to seek to establish herself as a writer in a public manner. The last two and a half decades of her life were lived out in the darkness and confusion of repeated mental breakdowns. Was Dorothy betrayed by her woman's body? Surely she herself, reticent and private, would have regarded the question as outrageous. Life with her brother William afforded her delicate, mobile perceptions, scope to flourish and a shelter that no one else could have given her. But the question remains of woman's body and whether it might betray the aspiring writer.

Women writers were much more literal than their male counterparts in their attachment to their own bodily being. Often, this was most striking in the images of maternity. While William Wordsworth pondered his somewhat abstract 'infant babe' nursed in maternal arms, drinking in through her 'the gravitation and the filial bond/ Of nature,' his precursor Mary Wollstonecraft, writing in May 1794 after the birth of her infant Fanny, rejoices in a literal 'inundation of milk'. (*Prel*.II:264-5; *WL*.255) She celebrates the bodily vitality of both mother and daughter: 'My little girl begins to suck so *manfully* that her father reckons saucily on her writing the second part of the R-ts of Woman.' (*WL*.256) The emphasis is on the young child, who she fondly hopes will surpass the mother.[7] When a year later she composes her *Letters from*

Sweden, Wollstonecraft reflects on the 'the enchantment of animation' as maternal nature echoes and sustains her own fecundity.[8] For Wollstonecraft after long struggle, the female body empowers rather than betrays.

The woman writer had to make sense in a way that permitted her both to nurture her infant and to grow into adult self-consciousness.[9] Where women writers were concerned, William Wordsworth's sense of 'that most apprehensive habitude' the child gained from its idealised mother, or Percy Shelley's 'obstinate questionings' of a 'Great Parent', however poignant the longing for a fit imaginative origin, were philosophical speculations, symbolic evasions if one will, of an inviolably physical condition. (*Prel.*II:256)[10]

The strong, literal questions had to do with survival. Women could and did die in childbirth and Wollstonecraft, who was killed by puerperal fever eleven days after giving birth to the infant Mary, is only the most celebrated literary example of what was a common enough fate. The theme of orphancy that runs like a dark, tangled thread through the writings of the three women considered here, has its basis not just in biographical fact but also in an imagination that had to struggle often in isolation, towards a mature, disciplined sense of what a female literary knowledge might be like.

While the quest theme vivified the writings of William Wordsworth and Percy Shelley, for Dorothy Wordsworth and Mary Shelley there were more substantial, less spiritual barriers in the way of desire. The exaltation of feeling prized by Romantics posed severe problems for women. However liberating, female desire was singularly hard to express. Women had to survive in a culture in which the search for personal fulfilment had no ready place. Small wonder then that Mary Wollstonecraft placed her heroine Maria in a prison for the insane, the better to cast into relief the terrible tension in a woman's mind resulting directly from her powerlessness. In her revolutionary *Vindication of the*

Rights of Woman (1792) she was careful to relate the ideal of 'JUSTICE for one-half of the human race' to her quarrel with patriarchy, its laws of primogeniture, its authority descending from kings and 'the king of kings'.[11]

Mary Shelley, though mindful of her mother's radical politics, veered sharply from an overt analysis of women's lot. Haunted by the ways in which genius had to accommodate itself to the demands of a culturally prescribed femininity, she presented a series of female figures, lovely and compliant, their powerlessness serving to clarify the limitless ambition of their men.[12] The daughter had to struggle with her mother's revolutionary feminism. In a journal entry of October 21, 1838, she wrote: 'with regard to "the good cause" – the cause of the advancement of freedom and knowledge, of the rights of women, etc. – I am not a person of opinions. That my parents and Shelley were of the former class, makes me respect it.' Yet she would not be thought heartless or lacking in compassion: 'If I have never written to vindicate the rights of women, I have ever befriended women when oppressed.'[13]

Mary Shelley declared that she was not for 'violent extremes' and found it impossible to push herself forward: 'I *cannot* do that; it is against my nature. As well cast me from a precipice and rail at me for not flying.' She voices the same strain of femininity in 1831 by distancing herself from the grotesque imaginings of her youthful self, the creation in *Frankenstein* of a pitiful, disfigured monster who turns violent in his outrage at human rejection: 'so very hideous an idea' she calls it.[14]

Woman's Labour: Writing and Mothering

With the grasp of the personal self, the intimate 'I' so critical to the literary reflections of the epoch, writing as a woman involved a tormenting contradiction. How could a being taught to govern her desires, mask over her longings in keeping with the claims of propriety, learn to unveil her silent self? How was it possible to cut through the bonds of femininity?

Each of the women considered in this book, while struggling with the painful tensions involved in female creativity, either overtly or in most secret and hidden ways, turned to her own physicality, discovering there a root of fresh imaginative knowledge. And part of that knowledge was the bond to other women and the cycles of generation.

Writing as a mother or a daughter, was female labour, involving a defining moral commitment. On the one hand was Mary Wollstonecraft, who right from the outset took to herself the didactic powers of maternity. Her very first work, was entitled in characteristic fashion *Thoughts on the Education of Daughters* (1787). On the other hand was her daughter Mary Shelley, haunted by a mother who died shortly after giving birth to her, the burden of maternal loss intensified by her own numbing experience of infant mortality. In contrast to Wollstonecraft's resolute turning towards the future, Mary Shelley's writing often displays a world so radically unstable that a future is hard to conceive of. The voice is overwhelmed by a past that cannot be recovered, and a future that might rupture all that the fragile present holds.

Time and again in Mary Shelley's work to be born is to be radically displaced. Orphancy is almost a precondition of bodily being. In 1820, still recovering from the death of her little son William, she uses her play *Proserpine* (1820) to examine the symbolic connection between female fruitfulness and natural plenitude. If nature, as the common figure held is female, and if woman's procreative powers are intimately involved with and analogous to the cycles of birth, death and renewal visible in the landscape, then maternal loss must equal natural devastation, and a mother's rage at the loss of her child can tighten and twist into a vision of universal destruction: 'Ceres for ever weeps, seeking her child And in her rage has struck the land with blight.'[15] The daughter Proserpine, stolen from her mother by the 'King of Hell' must suffer for having eaten of the forbidden pomegranate. Her sexual needs have cut her from her mother's kingdom. Echoing the phrase Shelley had used for Mary, Iris in the play ponders the lost child's identity: 'Art thou still, Proserpine, a child of light?' (P.35)

When Ceres threatens to cast the whole of created nature back into chaos, her ferocity prefigures the devastation Mary Shelley would visit on the human world in the novel she composed after Percy's death, *The Last Man* (1826). What would it be like if an outraged mother worked her vengeance and turned the 'fair world' into 'chaos once again'? The bare, contorted landscapes that Wollstonecraft conceived of in her unfinished *Cave of Fancy* return in heightened, even surreal form. The narrator of *The Last Man* inhabits a world where maternal nature can no longer support its creatures. The aged mother has turned into a 'harsh step-mother'.[16] Despair in the aftermath of failed revolutions, the ruin of warfare, fuses with the pain of Shelley's tragic death by drowning. Bit by bit, a plague for which there is no known cure, wipes out human civilisation.

But the beginning of *The Last Man* invokes female labour essential to the physical existence of the work. The text, the narrator declares, is fashioned from fragments of leaf and bark filled with curious inscriptions, which she and her companion had discovered in a dark, Sybilline cave: a history recovered from the womb of time.

For the woman writer an enforced marginality as far as the practicalities of literary production were concerned could often be best imaged as a painful lack of mothering. To lack a mother's love is to lack a place in the world, a theme that Wollstonecraft used first in *Maria, Or the Wrongs of Woman* (1798). Maria's unjust incarceration forces her to question a world in which woman, by the very nature of her being, is forced into marginality. But the novel as a whole is based not on the premise of solitude, but on the bond with new life with the infant daughter so cruelly torn from Maria. Her maternal body suffers. Her breasts are 'bursting with the nutriment for which this cherished child might now be pining in vain'.[17] She struggles to read but grief wells up. The mother's passionate life overwhelms the constructs of reason: 'Tears of maternal tenderness obscured the reasoning page.' (*MWW*.81) She turns to writing, to unburden herself, addressing herself to the child she hopes is still living and might one day survive to read her memoir. Maria must instruct her child, in order to save herself from madness.

Jemima the prison warder tells of a childhood robbed of a mother's love:

> I cannot help attributing the greater part of my misery, to the misfortune of having been thrown into the world without the grand support of life – a mother's affection . . . I was an egg dropped on the sand; a pauper by nature, hunted from family to family, who belonged to nobody – and nobody cared for me. (*MWW*.106)

But the act of writing could be cathartic. Even as it played out the themes of orphancy and displacement, it permitted a momentary poise, a balancing act. This is perhaps most acutely visible in the writings of Dorothy Wordsworth. All that she saw and marked in her fleeting perceptions, finely modulated to language, was visibly provisional, haunted by a sense of possible disappearance. Through a series of strategic displacements on to the landscape, emotion was distanced from the feminine self. The writer retained her seemingly inviolable privacy. Yet it was precisely this privacy which stood at risk in the nurturing acts of femininity that Dorothy valued so greatly. Although she never bore children, almost all of Dorothy's adult life was spent as a second mother, an aunt to William and Mary's children. She was intimately concerned with what it meant to mother.

In *Mary Jones and her Pet Lamb* (1805) Dorothy implicitly ponders how maternal care might be renewed and restored, how essential it is to survival. The more mature rendering of a Grasmere tragedy *George and Sarah Green* (1808) takes as its central theme the death of parents. The early death of William and Dorothy's mother and the splintering of their family of origin, together with her intense sympathy for her brother William, led her to choose a life with him, effectively foreclosing the possibility of marriage and child-bearing.

Renunciation leads to the utter annihilation of substance in her poem 'Floating Island'. The poem in which the tiny slip of land, torn free of the maternal coast and condemned to vanish by an arbitrary and capricious nature (towards which the speaking voice is careful to display no animosity) exhibits many of the same characteristics of her other writings: a concern with displacement, mutability and annihilation. And sometimes in the face of it all, a precarious, illuminating joy.

Appearance for Dorothy Wordsworth, even as it hinges on the visible landscape, displays little of the centralising hold of the Romantic 'I' so familiar in the poetry of her brother William. A means of knowing emerges in her writing, akin to the subtle quietness that was appreciated in women – a feminised knowledge if one will – non-confrontational, valuing the present and the boundaries of discrete and palpable phenomena, concerned too with care giving and nurture, anxious not to enter into the realms of overt power. Yet the pain of such a life was never far from the surface in her work. Gaining precision and refinement through the renunciation of male-identified power, she exemplifies at its finest one possible female response to the call of Romanticism.

The contrast with her predecessor Mary Wollstonecraft could not be greater. For Wollstonecraft writing was inconceivable apart from the battle to redefine the arena of feminine activity. Often it was as if in order to exist she had to appear in the public world – to publish – and between her fierce, all consuming activity of writing and the fact of publication, there was scarcely a gap. For Dorothy Wordsworth, bound to the intimate privacy of her life with William and sharing in his circle of literary friends, publication did not really seem necessary. When forced to the test by her friend Catherine Clarkson who urged her to publish *George and Sarah Green*, Dorothy was clear that she must preserve the silence both of her life and that of the orphans whose story she was telling. To at least one of her contemporaries, it seemed as if the 'nervous depression' to which she succumbed in the last two and a half decades of her life, was at least partially the result of her refusal to take up 'the profession of authorship'.[18]

But Wollstonecraft's strategy also had its difficulties. Often for her it was as if not to publish, were not to exist. And the necessity was not merely economic. It was rooted in her sense of herself. Her life was corroded by the insecurities that can sometimes befall a revolutionary existence, and her writing might well have improved had she been able to distance herself from it. But it seems mean spirited to ask of her what was surely a luxury, given the pressures of her ordinary life, a woman who had to rethink the world even as she wrote, struggling to save her 'soul alive'.

The phrase sounds as if it comes from Mary Wollstonecraft. It was inspired by the portrait that John Opie painted of her, hung now in the National Portrait Gallery. Visiting London over a century after Mary Wollstonecraft's death, a traveller from America gazed at the portrait. Ruth Benedict tells of how she was struck by the auburn hair of the woman in the picture, the 'sad steady' light of the eyes: 'I wanted so desperately to know how other women had saved their souls alive.' In Wollstonecraft she recognises a woman who had succeeded. 'She *had* saved her soul alive; it looked out from her steady eyes unafraid. The price too that life had demanded of her was written ineradicably there.'[19]

1 Romantic Feminine

Blake: 'This Shining Woman'

An often subtle, sometimes brutal tension between imaginative power and the claims of femininity marked the writing of women in the Romantic epoch. 'Every Eye Sees differently As the Eye – Such the Object', wrote Blake in one of his best known aphorisms, locating the source of truth for Romantic man in the complicated realm of the individual subjectivity.[1] Blake's intense celebration of the power of visionary desire lacked the universality he himself might have claimed for it. This exciting, potent ideal could not be translated into female imagination without great difficulty and danger.

For women writers of the epoch, the evolving mythology of the powerful Romantic self, only laid bare the cultural constraints implicitly barring women from the intensity Romantics celebrated. Woman as a precious object for the male gaze was defined primarily in terms of appearance. And I speak of appearance here not merely in terms of the flourishes of dress and bodily comportment, or the highly valued qualities of silence, simplicity and nurturance, but in the stricter sense of appearing for consciousness: how one appears, indeed how one gains permission to appear.

The problem of appearance as it afflicts the feminine, was recognised by Blake. His *Book of Thel* (1789) presents a young woman haunted by the transitory nature of her own self. All that she can compare herself to are creatures that vanish, figures predicated on their own transience: 'a reflection in a glass', 'shadows in water', 'dreams of infants'. (*B*.3) Lacking the power to unlock her own desires she can only long for easeful death. Yet she is driven by forces beyond her conscious awareness to seek meaning in the dark, entangled underworld of the senses. Unable to reconcile her 'shining' femininity to the kingdom of her tormented bodily desires, Thel flees in terror. Thel's unnaturally prolonged innocence cannot serve her, and Blake shows his readers how unfit she is for the knowledge of experience. She must survive if she can in an experiential limbo, her exquisite femininity ill suited to life:

> And all shall say, without a use this shining woman liv'd,
> Or did she only live to be at death the food of
> worms. (*B*.5)

Thel's poignant complaint echoes through the expressive lives and works of women of the epoch who were unable to strike free into the uncharted realms of female experience, what Wollstonecraft in *Mary, A Fiction* (1788) called 'a new world'.

The denial of female sexuality, whether through the oppression of a patriarchal order, or through woman's internalisation of that order finds potent expression in Blake's poetry. In 'A Little Girl Lost' he writes of innocent Ona after her sexual dalliance in the garden of earthly delights, shivering under her father's tormented gaze. This confrontation between a daughter's desire and a father's repressed longing, touches on a chord that Mary Shelley was to intensify in her 1819 novella, *Mathilda*. But while Blake's Ona has already loved her young man, and must stand trembling in guilt and perhaps hidden rage at her father's knee, Mary Shelley's Mathilda is consumed by desire for her father. Mathilda loves her father, in part but not in the whole, so that she might almost literally incarnate the mother who died to give her birth. By fulfilling her father's desire, she might as it were, rebirth herself. But such access to a better world was impossible. The patriarchal power implicit in the father, in all fathers in the Romantic era, could scarcely be combated through overt desire. Indeed, weaker almost than Blake's Ona, Mathilda must claim the powers of feminine subterfuge to survive. Her very self becomes what Adorno was to call a 'negative imprint of domination'.[2]

Yet a curious power lies in wait for her, one that is intimately connected to the covert nature of the feminine self in a culture that could not grant it a ready fulfilment of sexual desire. In Blake's poem 'The Sick Rose' the feminine flower shields its longing. It is gnawed from within by a phallic 'invisible worm'. Sickness invades the blossom, consuming its 'bed/Of crimson joy'. (*B*.23)

In her play with death, with the powers of darkness that invade the realm of desire, Mary Shelley's Mathilda was acting out a theme that had intense power for Blake. As a woman writer, and a second generation Romantic, sceptical of the possibilities of imaginative and social redemption, she could not easily distance herself from the consumption she imaged. Mathilda's death is an excess overflowing the boundaries of the text, erasing the distances between author and heroine.

With his vision of the Contraries that underwrite the whole of existence, his anarchic mythologies and his radical political sympathies, Blake of all the English Romantic poets best portrays female desire. Yet not even Blake can fully save himself from the patriarchal postures he so condemns. Women as complex, compulsive objects of his sexual gaze, whether we think of the Little Girls Lost or Oothoon, are surely physical even at times revolutionary beings, but never beings compelled to go a step further and write their lives into meaning. Nowhere in Blake do we find a woman both sexual and a bard.

Pushed to its end point, desire can only recoil on the feminine consciousness: there is no world as yet to receive it. While there is no doubt a tragic, truthful point here about the nature of the social world and the oppressed state of women, one must also point out that for William Blake the feminine, however much it might wish to be in and for itself, exists primarily in order to minister to the creative dynamism of the masculine.[3]

There is a world of difference between Blake's tragic feminine figures struggling to free themselves from a derivative existence, and the torment of a woman writer like Mary Wollstonecraft, who must cut herself loose of the bonds of femininity even as she recreates herself in writing. The concern in this chapter with images of femininity in Blake, Wordsworth and Shelley can only partially prepare us for the complex, often involuted strategies of women writers who had to confront, contort or set aside, each in her own fashion, the previously given visions of knowledge and power.

Romantic Inwardness

In his *Dialogue on Poetry* (1799) Friedrich von Schlegel points out how the agony of Romantic poets was the direct result of a lack of 'mythology', a shared body of belief that might sustain the imagination providing 'a matrix, a sky, a living atmosphere'.[4] It seemed to him that the only way was for each poet to construct his unique vision, a 'mythology' in Schlegel's words that was like no other, based in the individual consciousness. Schlegel was well aware that such a strategy would lead to a multitude of 'mythologies', each created by the individual poet 'like a new creation out of nothing'.

With inwardness as the source of a fresh 'mythology', external reality had to reflect human emotion. In *De l'Allemagne* (1810, 1813), Mme de Staël speaks of how an internalised life requires the transformation of nature: 'in order to serve as the emblem of his [man's] thoughts, nature must magnify itself in human eyes'.[5]

The result was a concern with metamorphosis, with the capacity of symbols to embellish the external world with the nuances of inner life. Coleridge, drawing on German thought, even copying out chunks of it, confirms in his notion of the Imagination (a central faculty through which subjectivity was affirmed) that it 'dissolves, diffuses, dissipates, in order to recreate'.[6] For Hegel, this fluidity of imaginative power transforms the world into an endless series of metamorphoses, and becomes a fierce, addictive, posture. In the introduction to his *Philosophy of Fine Art* he writes of how inwardness which for him constitutes the essence of the romantic, 'celebrates its triumph over the external world'.[7]

The feminine had a very special place in Romantic imagination. Drawn into the work and charged with symbolic power, the feminine was still linked in however elliptical a fashion to the actual lives of women. And women were real human beings, endowed with self-consciousness, capable both of inspiring and thwarting the designs of the poets.

It was here that the Romantic powers of myth-making came into full play. In a paradox that can only be sustained in the erotic imagination or in poetry, Romantics construed the feminine both as an otherness to which desire could be directed, and as an image within the work, mobile, metamorphic, precisely in keeping with poetic impulse.[8] As if in fulfilment of Schlegel's notion of a personal mythology, each poet absorbed the idea of the feminine into a new poetic universe.

To the Romantic, according to Mario Praz, woman was source both of beauty and corruption. The poet was fascinated by the cruelty projected out of his own desire, and the feminine with beauty and death commingled, turned into 'a sort of two-faced herm filled with corruption and melancholy and fatal in its beauty'.[9] While one need not go so far as Praz in this argument from necrophilia, it seems clear that Romantic inwardness waged its battle with the otherness of woman, placated only when consciousness had either satisfactorily absorbed into itself the valued qualities of femininity, or when visionary desire had rendered woman an object, sublime perhaps, but an object nevertheless for its fierce, appetitive force.

But there is a more positive aspect to the Romantic feminine. Drawing on the sentimental tradition, enlarging it, Romantics redefined the limits of moral knowledge. They drew on the powers of intense feeling, empathy and nurturing care. This was implicitly a validation of femininity and the functions previously reserved for women.[10] A revolutionary age needed to provide its own visible indices for the longing for change, and the feminine could at times satisfactorily stand in for this longing.

The focus on the masculine privileges of Romantic subjectivity – taken into poetry as an epistemological right, the right to know, the right to make meaning – turns into that overweening emphasis on the personal self most visible in Wordsworth. Keats was to dub this enlarged, mythical self the 'Wordsworthian or egotistical sublime'.[11]

For Wordsworth the feminine granted sympathy, infused feeling into a mental activity that might otherwise have lacked real contact with life. In his poetry he placed a very high value on the nurturing and domestic functions of women. The problem for Dorothy was how best to reconcile the nurturing, sisterly role she accepted, a role that her brother needed her to assume, while at the same time strengthening the conflicting, autonomous powers of her genius.

In Shelley's poetry woman, threatening in her otherness,

is transformed both in 'Alastor' and 'Epipsychidion' into a most precious figment of the poet's imagination. Almost literally, she is projected out of his consciousness only to have her being burnt up in the intensity of visionary desire. Shelley's idealised feminine participated in the same imaginative force that led him to conceive of absolute sexual freedom for both men and women, as part of a new world of revolutionary justice. But the ideal feminine was a play of his own imagination, a figuration of intense desire. The poet's union with her burns up his mind.

A male poet's vision, even as it serves to bring feminine values into the realm of poetry, presents women writers with the problem of remaking femininity. Only then could it become part and parcel of female genius, portion of a moral knowledge drawn from woman's 'original source'. (*MWW*. Advertisement)

Haunted in the early days of her writing career by the need to grant meaning and value to woman's existence, Wollstonecraft conceived of her first novel *Mary, A Fiction*, as an attempt to create a heroine whose powers were drawn not from the realm of the feminine as commonly defined by 'opinion' but 'by the individual from the original source'. The confrontation with Romantic visions of the individual self could not be avoided.

In trying to recover an 'original source' for women, Wollstonecraft wished to outstrip the power of the second-hand or male icon of the feminine. But how could this new, female imagination be imaged? How could it be grasped? The sheer difficulty of her task is visible in *Maria*. In the heroine's cruel incarceration we see a breakdown of her struggle for freedom. But it is also a coming to ground, a true beginning. Jailed by the strictures of an unjust society, Maria is freed in spirit to question the very nature of life as she has lived it. The instability of her voice, the terror that befalls it, are figured in the plight of the insane who surround her. As the narrative voice tells it, contemplation itself turns 'giddy, and we fearfully ask on what ground we ourselves stand'. (*MWW*.84)

Wollstonecraft, clearly subversive where the norms of society were concerned, was as powerfully inspired as Blake by the revolutionary ideals of her age. The world had to be remade in accordance with the claims both of individual desire and social justice. But desire is bounded by gender, by the social construction of sexuality. Male and female are unequal in the range of possibilities they are offered. For Wollstonecraft the conflict with male dominance was inevitable. Where a female consciousness as acute and unafraid as hers, comes into conflict with the centralising goals of Romantic knowledge, feminism most clearly emerges. For Dorothy Wordsworth the conflict was more secret, more hidden. The intense passion that bound her to her brother William, rendered unstable any possible feminism on Dorothy's part. Wordsworth's cult of individual genius effectively inhibited any conflicting momentum on her part. The strategies she evolved for going her own way as a woman writer are cause for both wonder and celebration. They were fragile, however, and could not last long. In that respect we can say of Dorothy Wordsworth that her life overwhelmed her imaginative resilience.

Elusive Feminine

In the poetry of William Wordsworth, even as nature is feminised, providing a context almost maternal for the imaginative transactions of the poet's consciousness, the figures of actual women whether a tragic bereaved mother or a quiet, contemplative sister, provide the voice with a sustenance that serves to heighten its intrinsic solitude, an acute centering of self. In 'Lines composed a few miles above Tintern Abbey, on revisiting the Banks of the Wye during a Tour. July 13, 1798' a poem that was to abide with

Dorothy Wordsworth in her tragic decline, the figure of the sister emerges only in the very last stanza of the poem. She stands as a stay against dissolution, an icon of the poet's past, a delicate double whose 'wild eyes' must mirror precisely the intensity the speaker cherishes in himself. Listening to his words, she validates both his physical being ('when like a roe/ I bounded o'er the mountains') and his sad, meditative genius. He wants nothing less of her than that she should bear his unique subjectivity, imprinted now into her own, into a realm of life surpassing his death.

To achieve an intimation of immortality through his younger sister, seemed, within the construct of one of his finest poems, a matter wholly conceivable. For she was taken into him almost as a double, another distinguished from the self by sex and youth, turning her into one who can listen and learn.[12] While it is difficult to doubt the acute, pained love the poet bears for his sister, it is equally difficult from a feminist perspective not to acknowledge the sister's symbolic presence as subservient to both genius and desire, gaining power precisely insofar as she is gathered into his vision.

In his 'Home at Grasmere' (1800–6), Wordsworth celebrates the bliss of his life with 'Emma' (a code-name for Dorothy), the domestic harmony she ensures protecting the high 'Power' of poetry. Yet she is herself a most elusive creature, valued quite precisely as she vanishes. She enters consciousness through a series of elisions, haunting in themselves, inviting the reader to question her presence. Her companionship, most precious when unseen, is likened to 'a flash of light' or 'a breath/Or fragrance independent of the wind'. Her voice most acute when she is unseen is like 'a hidden Bird that sang'.[13]

Later in the poem, the speaker discovers that the lovely pair of swans, emblem surely of his and Emma's companionship, have vanished from the valley. The abrupt loss heightens the subtraction from the physical that Emma's feminine elusiveness had already hinted at. The path is clear now for the poet's imagination to grasp itself as a power akin to that of the valley: 'a Centre . . . without dependence or effect'. (*HG*.49) And the existence of Others is left hanging in the air, glimpsed through the haunting, ultimately unanswerable questions the speaker puts to himself:

'Why do *They* shine around me, whom I love?
Why do they teach me, whom I thus revere?
Strange question, yet it answers not itself.' (*HG*.95)

Having affirmed the 'internal brightness' that belongs to the poet alone, the voice ponders 'humble Roof' and 'calm fireside', indices of shelter and domestic contentment and finds them inadequate. The emphasis on solitary grandeur, the Wordsworthian version of the Romantic will to power, follows closely on: 'Possessions have I that are solely mine,/Something within which yet is shared by none – /Not even the nearest to me and most dear.' (*HG*.95) In order to gain territory, to spread itself out through the world, the poet's power nurtured and nourished by his Emma's love, must paradoxically be sealed off from her, deep within the mythic recesses of a unique subjectivity.

Yet it is clear in the poem that the feminine has played its part in securing this centrality for the poet. Validating his adult choice of a home, his beloved Emma ('younger Orphan of a Home extinct/The only Daughter of my Parents') allows the poet both to satisfy and transcend whatever nostalgia for a lost home he might once have possessed. (*HG*.43) Still this is just a prelude, a preparation for the freedom of the poet, his powers intense, intensely solitary and wide-spreading. But without the tender address to his beloved sister, her physical presence fluently refined out of the here and now, the fierce knowledge of poetic singularity would have been much harder if not impossible to come by. She sustains his intimate self, serving almost as she had done in 'Tintern Abbey' as a stay against a grown man's solipsism.

*   *   *

The physical, bodily basis of Wordsworthian knowledge is established early in *The Prelude*. The keen awareness of the physical edges of things, critical to Wordsworth's poetic ability, was conceived, not within the processes of mentality but in actual experience, through what Dorothy Wordsworth called 'the evidence of the senses'. The skating scene in Book 1 of *The Prelude* offers an apt example.[14] Triumphant in his prowess, the young boy wheels about on the ice 'Proud and exulting, like an untired horse/That cares not for its home.' His bodily skills allow the child to map out the world around him, enter into it in a spontaneous, unreflective act. The prerogative of territory is taken for granted; with his companions the young boy acts out the dangers, the incipient violence of the hunt. Yet the 'alien sound/Of melancholy' sent in from the far off hills, prepares us for the meditative withdrawal, the summoning up of inwardness, the cutting apart of the young child's self so that even as he stands stock still after his wild and whirling motion on the ice, the cliffs, even the very earth still spins, stretching out as spectacles for consciousness: 'Feebler and feebler, and I stood and watched,/Till all was tranquil as a dreamless sleep.' (*Prel*.1:459, 470-1, 488-9)

From bodily immersion, sheer, unreflective action the child has moved to an intuitive grasp of his own conscious power. In the next stanza the sublimity latent in the scene – the boy has left the tumult of his friends to 'cut across the image of a star/That gleamed on ice' – is drawn out, as the adult voice of the poet invokes the 'presences of Nature' that mark out the visible terrain with 'the characters of danger or desire.' Clearly though, the 'ministry' of nature, haunting the young child in order to educate him, is co-extensive, at least at the early, formative stages of childhood with the marks of the child's own desire, the very brink of his power shot through with unearthly knowledge.

We see too how the landscape once the vital, solid correlative to the child's active self, is transformed for the meditating consciousness into a visionary spectacle, the centre of consciousness holding sway, turning, as Wordsworth so desired, into a power like Nature's. Rousseau's dictum in Book 2 of *Émile* that the boy child might learn through bodily activity, through the actual experience of his physical power ('we men are made for strength') receives its poetic exemplification. (*E.*111) Skirmishing with danger, here the bruises and blows inflicted by a flying ball, Rousseau's Émile, like Wordsworth's boy child learns his own strength.

'I know of nothing sublime which is not some modification of power.' Edmund Burke had written in his influential work *A Philosophical Enquiry into The Sublime and Beautiful* (1757).[15] Terror for Burke underlies the sublime, and with it comes an instinctive sense of human vulnerability, a simultaneous withdrawal from and fascination with what is awe-inspiring, even violent and dangerous in its claims on our own selves. The feminine however is clearly distinguished from this perceived source of power: it is small, delicate, pleasing to the eye in its proportions. It seems to Burke quite clear that 'the beauty of women is considerably owing to their weakness, or delicacy, and is even enhanced by their timidity, a quality of mind analogous to it'. (*SB.*116) The feminine then must be held quite clear of all that goes into the welter of power defining sublimity. That which is worthy of love – as opposed to admiration, and Burke's thoughts here fit in with his perception of the feminine – must submit 'to us'. His thought, aphoristic in its tautness, is quite clear: 'we submit to what we admire, but we love what submits to us'.

His thoughts on feminine weakness are in agreement with Rousseau's sense in *Émile* that while men might learn the limits of their bodily power in the rough and tumble of childhood play, women must preserve their decorous weakness: 'Kite-flying is a sport for women, but every woman will run away from a swift ball. Their white skins were not meant to be hardened by blows . . . ' (*E*.111) Lest it be thought that I am arguing for all women to play the dreaded ball games, I hasten to add that Rousseau's desire to preserve women from hardship is not as innocuous as it seems. In his overweening concern with feminine appearance, he prevents the girl child from taking up the unseemly, empowering act of writing.

If all that is great, terrible and awe-inspiring, and hence a fitting source for what is conceived of as poetic genius must be cut apart from what is fine boned, small and beautiful, the realm of the feminine, it is hard to see what scope femininity might have for the productions of genius. A gendered world, then, grants the feminine a unique and differentiated status: not power but delicacy, not genius but its domestication, not sublimity but the hold on the near at hand and common.

For women writers of the period, the kinds of imaginative power that a male writer could assume – access to the public world, the centrality of the imaginative self, however tormented and tortuous its self-definition – could scarcely be taken for granted. The traditional division of spheres, with the realms of public power, volition and accomplishment reserved for men and the arena of the private and domestic reserved for women, underlay the configurations of imaginative knowledge in the Romantic era.

*　　*　　*

For Wordsworth the strategy of using a feminine double to male genius was deeply rooted in the stuff of his day to day life. In Percy Shelley's work however, the feminine double is cut entirely free of the hold of the familial and tender. It turns abstract, ethereal, a figment of desire projected out of the poet's own psyche. In poems like 'Alastor' and 'Epipsychidion', the feminine figure conveys both the burning intensity and the literal impossibility of desire.

The ill-fated Narcissus sought his own image. Shelley's Alastor seeks out a feminine figure, her distinct being eerily fitted to his own. Her voice 'was like the voice of his own soul/Heard in the calm of thought.'[16] The speaker informs us that she too is a poet, a fact which enables her to echo back in seemingly impossible perfection, each impulse of his thought. The 'veiled maid' who has come to the poet in a 'vision' is thus clearly preferable to the Arab maiden of the previous stanza, who for love of Alastor steals out from her father's tent bearing him food. Her utter devotion to him, her wordless love is clearly unrequited.

The visionary woman has no commerce with the world of bodily necessity. The purity of her mind is such that it 'kindled through all her frame/A permeating fire'. Beneath the seductive and sinuous veil, the poet sees 'by the warm light of their own life/Her glowing limbs.' But their embrace entails a burning annihilation, the impossible object of desire, projected from the poet's consciousness, plunging him into the abyss of an orgasmic end.

> He reared his shuddering limbs and quelled
> His gasping breath, and spread his arms to meet
> Her panting bosom . . .
> Now blackness veiled his dizzy eyes, and night
> Involved and swallowed up the vision. (S.75)

In his Preface to the poem, Shelley describes the youthful Alastor as a creature of 'uncorrupted feelings and adventurous genius' drawn forwards through an imagination so intense, so 'inflamed and purified' that the world as it is can offer no hope. While the repeated images of burning convey both the sexual motive of this quest, as well as its literal impossibility – purity sought and maintained through a radical consumption – Shelley's own aims are satisfied insofar as Alastor's desires 'point towards objects thus infinite and unmeasured.' Still mere objects lose their power to enthrall and Alastor longs for an 'intelligence' akin to his own. 'He images to himself' Shelley writes in his Preface 'the Being whom he loves.' (S.69-70)

The path is laid for the projection of a feminine image whose existence far from being rooted in woman's bodily being, arises solely out of the male poet's imagination. While 'the lasting misery and loneliness of the world' forms part of Shelley's ever present theme – a here and now in which genius can never find its true counterpart – his visionary desire is so staunchly situated in his own uniqueness that a female other, however fascinated by his vision, must inevitably react against it if she is in search of her own autonomous sources of creativity.

It is possible to see in Mary Shelley's *Frankenstein*, in the obsessive Victor who creates another life out of his mental reckonings, a parodic rewriting of Alastor's quest. The grotesque being first abandoned, and then closely shielded by Victor as his own dark secret, stands as a fleshly obverse to Alastor's veiled maid. Instead of being pure spirit, a perfect counterpart to the poet's desire, it is irreducible flesh and blood, however cruelly deformed in body; never to be swallowed back into sheer consciousness.

In 'Epipsychidion' (1821) what the narrator tellingly alludes to as 'the brief fathom-line of thought or sense' can barely plumb the intensity of a quest for ideal love. (S.376) Emilia Viviani, the long sought beloved, perfect embodiment of the Vision that has long haunted the speaker, is herself just barely human. Her dissolution

from the bonds of mortality is essential if the ideal is
to persist in the face of suffering:

> Seraph of Heaven! too gentle to be human,
> Veiling beneath that radiant form of Woman
> All that is insupportable in thee
> Of light, and love, and immortality! (*S*.374)

The poem's title, coined from the Greek, means upon or
of the soul, an apt term for a work whose central theme is
the quest for a beloved, 'this soul out of my soul.' (*S*.379)
Prefiguring the poem in his essay *On Love*, composed in
the summer of 1818, Shelley ponders the essential apartness
of the beloved, whose being must necessarily transcend
'the chasm of an insufficient void' man discovers within
himself. Even as in a note to the essay he spells out the
radical insufficiency of words ('These words are inefficient
and metaphorical – Most words so – No Help – '), Shelley
attempts to describe this radiance: 'A mirror whose surface
reflects only the forms of purity and brightness: a soul
within our soul that describes a circle around its proper
Paradise which pain and sorrow and evil dare not overleap.'
(*S*.473, 474)

   Wordsworth's belief in 'a dark inscrutable workmanship'
permitted him to embed joy in the difficulties and trials of
the human world, the world in which love must be sought
and guilt endured. But for Shelley the purity of desire
was of such intensity and so unaccountable in the chaos
of phenomenal existence that only a Platonic separation
of actual and ideal could maintain its inexplicable glory.
For Wordsworth the centre of subjectivity is a clearly
defined 'I' which has speculative power over the world
of all imaginings, an 'I' to which the feminine, however
beloved, can only exist as complement. For Shelley both
self and feminine other must be utterly consumed in an
excess of spirit.

Imagining an 'Elysian isle' where under the 'roof of blue Ionian weather' the poet and his beloved will start their long slow dissolution, Shelley builds up the erotic theme ('Our breath shall intermix, our bosoms bound') till the climax is reached. Desire, perfected in self-duplication, charges the verse in a fierce rhythm so that the aftermath, the falling away in despair, almost seems not to matter: 'Confused in passion's golden springs/. . . We shall become the same, we shall be one/Spirit within two frames, oh! wherefore two?' (S.387)

But such feasting off the other, in sexual, poetic, delight cannot long be sustained, and the moment of 'one annihilation' is not far. The feminine as purest symbol is intoxicating, fiery and finally in Shelley's vision a catalyst for the longed for self-combustion.

2 True Appearances

Thoughts on the Education of Daughters (1787)

The heroine of Mary Wollstonecraft's last, unfinished work *Maria or the Wrongs of Woman*, addresses her memoirs to her young child 'uncertain whether I shall ever have an opportunity of instructing you . . . ' Writing might overcome the distance that cuts the mother from her daughter, permitting the expression of truth garnered from a painful life. 'For my sake, warned by my example,' writes Maria, 'always appear what you are, and you will not pass through existence without enjoying its genuine blessings, love and respect.'(*MWW*.124) What does Maria mean when she counsels her child to appear as she is?

Clearly it was the belief in reason that permitted Mary Wollstonecraft, a true daughter of the Enlightenment here, to conceive of a whole new way in which women might be in the world, one that would undo the violence of social norms that required a simple, seemingly serene appearance in women, their lives moulded to the requirements of masculine power.[1] At the same time, for Mary Wollstonecraft, there was a way in which the true self, if one might call it that, was closer to the feelings of the heart than any mode of instruction or social norm could compel. It was this freed sensibility she wanted for Maria's daughter.

The theme of feminine appearance and its relation to a true self was fraught with difficulty for women in the Romantic epoch and went through variant, conflicting presentations in women's writing. It is a tribute to the seriousness and integrity of Wollstonecraft's thought that one can approach an answer to what Maria might have

35

meant by turning back full circle to her earliest work *Thoughts on the Education of Daughters* (1787). Drawing on her experiences with female education in the school she had set up in Newington Green, Wollstonecraft enters into the debate about women's self-presentation and ways in which the expressive body must mediate the truth of the heart.

Her book was written as a response to the numerous eighteenth-century works of courtesy and conduct literature, counselling women on how to behave in society. Dr John Gregory, for instance, in his celebrated treatise, *A Father's Legacy to his Daughters* (1774) counselled his daughters to both modesty and secrecy. Their mother being dead he places himself with full assurance in her place, the patriarchal posture lending itself without doubt or difficulty to this double task. Female life, the learned doctor argues, is filled wholly with suffering. His motherless daughters must not forget that only religion can alleviate their pain. Sorrow in this world must be borne by women 'in silence, unknown and unpitied', masked over by an appearance of 'serenity and happiness'.[2] His daughters would do well to realise that the world cares only for the mask of tranquil femininity.

In marked contrast to the secrecy and decorum Dr Gregory prescribed, Wollstonecraft struggles to preserve female dignity, to discover a 'stay for the mind'.[3] Just twenty years old, she writes here as a woman to other women, using the pronoun 'we', her emotional involvement palpable even as the formalities of her chosen diction work to displace any overt show of feeling: 'How many people are like whitened sepulchres, and careful only about appearances! Yet if we are too anxious to gain the approbation of the world we must often forfeit our own.' (*T*.31)

The biblical undertones of her language, quite self-consciously utilised here, are part and parcel of her attempt to restore to women the human right of self-respect. It is in

order to please the world that women condemn themselves
to artifice, yet such simulated feeling is 'faint' or 'awkward'
when compared to real feeling. Accepting the demands of
propriety imposed on them, she argues that women have
'prostituted' their expressive powers, such that even the
'warmest professions of regard' can no longer be trusted.
(T.31) Her poignant plea for a woman to be seen 'as she
really is', while ignoring the complexities of emotional
conflict that she herself was so often prey to, reveals her
earnest desire to achieve some measure of self-respect for
her sex.

Going a step further, she argues for a beauty that only 'an
attention to the mind' can give. A 'well ordered mind' seems
the source of true bodily harmony. (T.33) Quite suspicious
of the passions, in this first work, the young writer argues
for clarity of mind. And since mind is mediated for the
world outside by women's bodily being, clothing is of
critical importance. Garments that are too 'glaring', that
might detract from attention paid to the woman's mind,
must be cast away.

The 'body', Wollstonecraft remarks, 'hides the mind
and it is, in its turn obscured by the drapery' (T.35)
yet just as proper clothing should in all suitable modesty
draw attention to the self, so the bodily self so long
distorted by the claims of vanity should purify itself
by incarnating mind. Hence body, though cover for
the mind, becomes alive with the inwardness it holds.
The familiar dualistic trope works for Wollstonecraft
here: embodiment gives the female mind entry into
the world, sets it in the world's eye rather than veil-
ing it.

And so all that would mask the given physicality of a
woman must be thrust aside: cosmetics for instance that
are smeared over the skin distort appearance, 'the whole
tribe of beauty washes, cosmetics, Olympian dew, oriental
herbs, liquid bloom . . . ' (T.38) Indeed such deception,

for that is how she views the excessive reliance on cosmetics, could prove dangerous to the woman: 'if caught
by it a man marries a woman thus disguised, he may
chance not to be wholly satisfied with her real person.'
(T.39) Wollstonecraft's fear was not wholly unfounded.
In 1770, Parliament had passed a bill declaring that a
woman who might 'seduce and betray into matrimony
any of His Majesty's subjects' would stand liable to the
penalty for witchcraft. The methods of such seduction and
betrayal are laid out quite clearly: 'scent, paints, cosmetics,
washes, artificial teeth, false hair, Spanish wool, iron stays,
hoops, high-heeled shoes, or bolstered hips'.[4] The contemporary anxiety with female appearance, indeed the fear of
desire itself, the female body and its possible deceptions
entrapping the vulnerable sexuality of the male, found in
the claims of propriety an ideal means of fixing woman,
setting her firmly in place. For Wollstonecraft wresting
an autonomous consciousness for woman meant a notional
separation of body from mind, granting women through the
tension of dualism, a painful, spiritual independence.

Reading Rousseau

The bond between physicality and symbolic expression
was of great concern to Romantics. Even if at times
they only gave their knowledge covert expression, the
Romantics were intensely aware of the ways in which
subjectivity was mediated by the bodily self. Writing was
itself an embodied act, holding the key to self-expression.
The powers it unlocked for the psyche could make feeling
bearable, transforming it into new meaning. This is why it
was critical for Wollstonecraft to cut through the cultural
requirements of femininity into the truths of the passionate
bodily self. Through apt instruction, women could be freed
from false control, taught – and here her Enlightenment

self comes into conflict with the Romantic exaltation of feeling – to reveal themselves as they truly were. Women could feel, act and change the world. Reading and writing were essential to this slow if substantial revolution in female morals.

Rousseau's account of the little girl shows us how critical appearance is to the self-intuitions of femininity. Her grasp of her own bodily self already mediated by the look of the other, the small girl prepares for womanhood. How else could she have determined that what she was doing was not 'pretty'? In that 'miniature fatherland, the home' there was no place for writing women. (E.326) Reading of how she catches sight of herself in the mirror, one recalls Sartre's analysis: 'I am in a world which the Other has made alien to me, for the Other's look embraces my being.'[5]

In her *Vindication of the Rights of Woman* (1792), Wollstonecraft lashes at Rousseau for his belief that 'woman ought to be weak and passive, because she has less bodily strength than man'. (V.173) The rationalism of the eighteenth century, the intellectual formation of her mentor Richard Price, fuses with the Romantic claims to truth through feeling, as Wollstonecraft moves to assert woman's rights to her own vision of the truth. The justice she sought for 'one half of the human race' meant moving away from self-mutilation. Romantic visions of the feminine had to be subjected to a fierce scrutiny. Rousseau whom she had praised for his 'uncommon portion of sensibility' (WL.145) was guilty where women were concerned.

To Rousseau it seemed perfectly evident that 'Nature herself has decreed that woman, both for herself and for her children, should be at the mercy of man's judgement'. (E.328) It followed that woman must 'naturally' desire to please man. Desirous of pleasing, she is also more capable than a man of enduring authority. While the young Émile could learn his place in life through the exercise of his own powers, Sophie, his intended, could only occupy herself by dressing her doll. 'This will not always be so; in due time she will be her own doll.' (*E*.331)

Wollstonecraft in her commentary is filled with pity. Sophie for her is a 'poor innocent babe' condemned to mimic the frippery around her. She must satisfy male desire, her 'limbs and faculties cramped with worse than Chinese bands'. The 'lifeless doll' she dresses is preparation for dressing her own body. (*V*.128) Indeed in constructing an appropriate set of surfaces for the male gaze she must practice a subtlety akin to what Dr Gregory had advocated.

Rousseau adds that Sophie's clothing was to be 'modest' seeming. But this was so that it could be taken apart 'bit by bit by the imagination'. (*E*.356, 357) Quick to the point, Wollstonecraft observes how specious it is to equate purity in women with covert acquiescence in a game of mental strip-tease. Her body annexed by the male gaze, powerless to fulfil her own desires, it is hardly surprising that the life of woman is what Rousseau says it is, 'a perpetual struggle against self'. (*E*.332) Her self-consciousness divided against itself, woman discovers a rupture at the very heart of subjectivity. One could even call it a shame unknown to male Romantics.

For Wollstonecraft, the image of prison surfaces again. Picking up on ideas first set out in *Thoughts*, she argues that mind trapped in a female body, confined to the realm of appearances, must necessarily atrophy. The mind 'shapes itself to the body, and roaming around its gilt cage, only seeks to adore its prison.' (*V*.131) Later the self is likened to a bird in a cage only able to 'plume and stalk with mock majesty.' (*V*.146) Now the female soul is firmly rooted in the body. There is no elsewhere, no land beyond the mind that can console and repair earthly pain, as there was in her first novel *Mary, A Fiction*. Consciousness is resolutely incarnate and must seek its fulfilment in this very world.

Her beloved Rousseau participated most powerfully in

the patriarchal vision of things. She does nothing to hide her anger: 'His ridiculous stories, which tend to prove that girls are *naturally* attentive to their persons, without laying any stress on daily example, are below contempt.' She implicitly links the confinement visited on young female children, such that they might seem 'naturally' to prefer dolls to active, bodily play with the vanity and concern for mere appearances that led the little girl to fling her pen away. And she pulls rank on Rousseau, pointing out her greater experience of female children: 'I have, probably, had an opportunity of observing more girls in their infancy than J.J. Rousseau.' (*V*.129)

While Mary, the heroine of Wollstonecraft's first fiction was able to write to ease the intensity of her pain and hold a splintering self together, for Rousseau's Sophie, bound to mere appearances, no words will ever work. No meaning, however fitful will redeem her woman's consciousness.

Authorship and the Mask of Femininity

Instead of living like 'whitened sepulchres', a phrase Wollstonecraft uses in *Thoughts*, women must discover an authentic self, capable of both action and expression. But this longing in her had to contend with the mask of femininity that women took to themselves to paper over the powerlessness of their daily lives. In *Mary, A Fiction*, the heroine's mother, seduced by the swooning femininity she discovers in the sentimental fiction of the day, thoroughly neglects her growing child. The young girl is left to fend for herself as the mother shares her bed with two lap dogs or imagines herself an actress in the torrid love scenes she devours. The writer is biting in her comment on Eliza: 'had she thought while she read, her mind would have been contaminated.' (*MWW*.3)

But lack of thought in no way prevents her from being

overpowered by the 'fatal image' of femininity that women must present if they are to ravish the male gaze. Occasional solitude instead of affording space for quiet reflection – which the daughter cherishes – leads the mother to attempt ever more rigorous approximations to the ideal of imagined bodily perfection.

As she was sometimes obliged to be alone, or only with her French waiting-maid, she sent to the metropolis for all the new publications, and while she was dressing her hair and could turn her eyes from the glass, she ran over those most delightful substitutes for bodily dissipation, novels. (*MWW*.2)

Given over to a worship of mere appearances, Mary's mother offers the perfect example of all that the young, rebellious girl has to slough off in order to enter the 'new world' of her own imagination. Yet that world, far from being fulfilled in her day to day life, drives Mary into torment. Bruised by passions that find no outlet in the shared world, the young woman in a pivotal scene in the novel discovers herself on board ship, utterly alone. Her beloved friend Ann is dead and Henry the sickly, sensitive violin player to whom she has transferred her affections, has parted from her. For two whole days, more than half in love with oblivion, Mary locks herself up in her cabin. But on the third night her intense anguished wakefulness thrusts her forward to save herself. Rocked by the waves, by the light of a small taper, she starts to write.

Her 'fragment', as Wollstonecraft calls it, is given to the reader as an explicit reminder of the graphic activity that provides the novel with its material existence. The fictive Mary struggling for psychic survival, fuses with her creator who has bequeathed her with her own name. The work fulfils the argument of its Advertisement that compositions that have the power to delight and captivate are those in which 'the soul of the author is exhibited'. The impulse to self-examination that underlies a good deal of her work, inspired Wollstonecraft to name the protagonists of both her novels with versions of her own. But while Maria, heroine of *Maria or the Wrongs of Woman*, was able for better and for worse to act out her own desires, the pre-revolutionary Mary is hemmed in on all sides.

In Romantic fashion, even as her fragment gives vent to anguish and isolation ('Poor solitary wretch that I am; here alone do I listen to the whistling winds and dashing waves; – on no human support can I rest . . . '), she knows that writing can still the intensity of feeling and blunt the edge of desire. A catharsis that most writers would welcome only hurts a woman who must endure a world that crosses out her desire. Dependent entirely on the torment within her to express her longing, she questions the relief that composition affords: ' "Father of Mercies, compose this troubled spirit: do I indeed wish it to be composed – to forget my Henry?" the *my*, the pen was directly drawn across in an agony.' (*MWW*.44)

The name of God the Father is invoked time and again; even Henry becomes as a 'father' to Mary. Subjectivity so constrained by the patriarchal world must be torn free. And so in the early stages of her writing career, like her creature Mary, Wollstonecraft was invaded by a constant, compulsive pain, the effort needed to cut through the bonds of her own feminine formation. A tormenting self-conflict often marked her reflections, a 'warfare' as she called it. In a letter of 1786 she offered a characteristic comment: 'I am often with myself at war – and forget the *shews* of love to other's – nay I cannot always feel alike.' (*WL*.110)

Yet however marked her ambivalence, others were often drawn into her life with its moments of intense self-dramatisation, as the public arena – that realm of visibility into which the estate of authorship cast her – played its part in the liberation of desire.

*   *   *

The ability to publish what she wrote was critical to her project of female self-definition. Publication by granting an objective form to personal knowledge could break open the hold of privacy and secrecy on the feminine, that gag to truth. Surely what was published, and I think of this as a hidden logic to her often feverish acts of writing, could partake of as profound a seriousness, as grave a prescriptive power as the minutiae of propriety, the codes of gender and hierarchical ordering that had so constrained women. It was even conceivable that female desire could underwrite a woman's relentless self-examination, turning pain into energy, loss into vital meaning.

Perhaps a tone of self-importance is audible in her early letter in which she announces to her sister Eliza: 'I *hope* you have not forgot that I am an Author'. But the voice continues with a characteristic honesty: 'yet many are the hours that are loaden with cares . . . I *ruminate* without digesting.' (*WL*.155) Five years later in 1792 after her name had gained public recognition and she was established as an author, Wollstonecraft wrote to her sister Everina from Paris. The poet and novelist Helen Maria Williams had greeted her 'very civilly', yet her manners seemed to the writer somewhat 'affected'. Though it pleased Wollstonecraft to note that 'the *simple* goodness of her heart continually breaks through the varnish', she added an astute observation: 'Authorship is a heavy weight for female shoulders especially in the sunshine of prosperity.' (*WL*.226) The public estate, even as it validated the female emotions, had to be guarded against, lest the very emotions it served to authenticate turn flaccid and corrupt in the social glare.

The woman writer as she struggles to grant a meaning and value to her days, has to think through the enticing if sometimes questionable nature of the public realm. The symbolic power of authorship highlights her conflicted inwardness, as the writer draws out the difficult consequences of seeking a place for her work in the shared world.

It was perhaps inevitable that she should seek to justify herself through the presumption of virtue. In the epigram from Rousseau with which *Mary* opens: 'L'exercice des plus sublimes vertues eleve et nourrit le genie,' Wollstonecraft subtly points out the task of self-nourishment that the woman writer had to come by. Later, in the Advertisement she pleads for 'the mind of a woman who has thinking powers.' We glimpse the tortuous strain of this argument: 'Without arguing physically about *possibilities* – in a fiction, such a being [a thinking woman] may be allowed to exist; whose grandeur is derived from the operation of its own faculties, not subjugated to opinion; but drawn by the individual from the original source.' (*MWW*.xxxi)

It was her daring project to conceive of a woman whose powers could be drawn from her own inwardness, without the mediation of the tight social world. For the male Romantic, the sense of self against world – a grandeur as Wollstonecraft thought of it – of sublimity in practical action seemed critical. An analogous sense of feminine creative power was hard to envisage. Indeed woman's own desire, located within *her* 'original source', could be singularly discomfiting, even threatening. And so right to the end of her life, Wollstonecraft struggled with Rousseau, whose subtle, pervasive sense of subjectivity as the centre of the interpreted world haunted her, even as her feminist self was revolted by his overt vision of female subservience.

In March 1787, during a time when her thoughts were often preoccupied with the themes of *Mary*, Wollstonecraft wrote to her sister Everina conveying her pleasure with *Émile*. Her comment pinpoints quite precisely the theme she had isolated in her choice of epigram to her novel, the ability of genius to educate itself: 'I am now reading

Rousseau's *Émile* and love his paradoxes. He chuses a *common* capacity to educate – and gives as a reason, that a genius will educate itself – however he rambles into that *chimerical* world in which I have too often wandered . . . ' (*WL*.145)

What is this 'chimerical world' that Wollstonecraft refers to? Her letter continues in partial explanation. Entry into such a world leads to the 'conclusion that all is vanity and vexation of spirit.' An elaboration of the phrase is brought out in her *Vindication* which was published five years later. In it, she writes of 'one of Rousseau's wild chimeras': women who are educated to be 'like a fanciful kind of *half* being.' (*V*.124) Her sentence occurs in the course of an argument concerning the only point of natural superiority that men possess over women, bodily strength. Yet the '*knowledge*' of women, Wollstonecraft asserts, is equal to that of men.

To buttress her argument, she sets out a long quotation from Book 5 of *Émile* in which Rousseau describes the education of Sophie and elaborates on the differences between men and women. The passage includes a phrase from Rousseau which must have been skimmed over by the younger self, thrust into the realm of the scarcely conscious. About women Rousseau writes: 'as for works of genius, they are beyond their capacity.' (*V*.124, *E*.350)

In order to read Rousseau, that 'strange inconsistent unhappy clever creature', in the years prior to her own radical awakening as a feminist, Wollstonecraft needed to cast aside her own femaleness, that potent sense of her own bodily self that could never be reduced into an illusory realm where women could only exist as surfaces for the male gaze. (*WL*.145) Such a casting aside or 'bracketing' of her female flesh in the interests of a higher knowledge, is reflected in the character of Mary, who at times seems to forget that she has bodily needs. It was years later, after her acknowledgement of her own ill-fated passion for Fuseli and spurred on by the tumult of the French Revolution, that Wollstonecraft turned to *Émile*, this time as a 'resisting reader', able to castigate Rousseau for his belief that a young girl's education, rather than forming her to live her own life, should fit her to please a male companion.[6]

Woman's Place (*Maria or the Wrongs of Woman*, 1798)

In the *Memoirs* (1798), composed after his wife's death William Godwin notes that the French Revolution caused a 'fundamental shock' in Wollstonecraft's system of thought, adding: 'the prejudices of her early years suffered a vehement concussion. Her respect for establishments was undermined.'[7] The great energy of moral change that was sweeping through radical England forced her to rethink the anger she had often turned inward at herself. The depression that sapped her, the 'warfare' that had no outlet except in death could be exchanged for a struggle directed at social conditions. (*WL*.128) In October 1786, entering the castle of the Kingsboroughs where she was to serve as governess, Wollstonecraft felt she was 'going into the Bastille'. (*WL*.120) Less than a week later she wrote of her anguish at teaching 'a heap of rubbish miss-called accomplishments'. She continues: 'I am grieved at being obliged to continue so wrong a system'. (*WL*.123-4)

With great political change visible across the horizon, might not the female faculties be recast, taught to question the very system they had once worked to perpetuate? Her authorial voice, publicly claimed in the wake of a people's agitation for social justice, tested itself against the patriarchal powers of Burke. Her emotional response to Burke's *Reflections on the Revolution in France* (1790) was dashed off in a 'glow of indignation', the very first to be printed.[8] The first edition appeared anonymously. Apparently mid-way through composing the work she lost nerve and it was only the publisher's offer to burn up the printed portions of the manuscript that impelled her forward. For a woman who wished 'to live independent or not live at all' (*WL*.199), it was a frightening but necessary step.

The female writer had come of age, her voice asserting a 'great end', the 'exercise of our faculties'. (*VRM*.29) Her passionate arguments attacked Burke's notion of hereditary property and primogeniture. She set the sacred, 'natural rights' of all men which 'prescription' could never undermine against the 'demon of property', her voice gathering power from the arguments of men like Tom Paine, the great revolutionary who had joined her circle of acquaintances. (*VRM*.8,22) She directed her personal outrage at the oppression of all those who had been disinherited by society: 'Hell stalks abroad', she wrote, ' – the lash resounds on the slave's naked sides'. (*VRM*.152) She sent a signed copy of her work to her mentor Richard Price, a man whom Burke had bitterly attacked in his *Reflections*.

Mary Wollstonecraft first met Richard Price in 1784 when she was setting up her school in Newington Green. It was a period crucial to her intellectual formation. His preaching in favour of the American Revolution opened her eyes to the claims of social justice and the belief in human perfectability. His emphasis on individual reason freed from hierarchical constraints appealed to the young woman who had always struggled to cut her own path through life. Price's notion of truth gave metaphysical sanction to her belief in social justice.

However elliptically the connections were made in her own mind, Wollstonecraft could move from internal 'warfare' and a world where 'the minute attention to propriety stops the growth of virtue' to questioning the political pre-conditions of that very world (*WL*.141). When Burke exhorted the public to pity Marie Antoinette who had seemed to him years earlier to glitter like the 'morning-star, full of life, and splendour, and joy' Wollstonecraft ridiculed him for lacking reason, for giving his voice over to the effeminacy of feeling.[9]

Yet in claiming a public voice the female author, almost despite herself, played into the given perceptions of masculine and feminine. Burke the patriarch is given to the feminine play of feeling and hence not to be seriously considered, while she takes the more virile 'masculine' intelligence based on reason. Her symbolic cross-dressing works into the attack on Burke. He suggested that female beauty rested on littleness and weakness. (SB.113,116) In a prefiguration of her second Vindication she argues such a notion deforms women. Unable to exercise reason – their very existence governed by a need to titillate the male eye – they have no access to virtue. 'You have clearly proved', she addresses Burke directly, 'that one half of the human species, at least, have not souls.' (VRM.113)

Excited by the public reception of her reply to Burke – her authorship once known was greeted both with scorn and praise – Wollstonecraft readied herself for the woman question, an issue more intimate, more painful than an attack on the establishment. Previous authors arguing for women's rights had confined themselves primarily to issues of education. But as a woman who had publicly found her voice, she might strip apart the condition of women imprisoned in their own vanity. Her writing would be strong and without a hint of 'sex' – nothing feminine about it. It would not be passive, pleading, titillating to the male reader. It would be an inscription like Catherine Macaulay's and as 'strong and clear'. (V.206)

Wollstonecraft's admiration for Catherine Macaulay's Letters on Education (1790) cannot be underestimated. It was a work she had reviewed and was clearly indebted to in formulating her own vision of feminism. Catherine Macaulay was the very first in eighteenth-century England to call out for a system of education that would be the same for both male and female.[10] Prefiguring the title of Wollstonecraft's celebrated work, Macaulay had wanted nothing less than a 'vindication of female nature'.[11] Her attack on Burke's notion of female beauty and her contempt for Sophie's behaviour in the influential *Émile* were both picked up by Wollstonecraft. Macaulay believed in freeing the bodily powers of young girls. 'Our sons,' wrote Macaulay, commenting on the energy natural in young children, 'may follow unmolested, those strong impulses which nature has wisely given.' She sees a sad inhibition in the case of young girls who showing off 'locomotive tricks in a manner not entirely agreeable to the trammels of custom' are sharply reproved and then are reined in with a severity that forces 'a consciousness of having highly transgressed the laws of decorum'. (*LE*.47)

In Catherine Macaulay, Wollstonecraft had discovered a forebear who believed that knowledge was the just object of life, that virtue in both sexes was identical, in short that truth could not be portioned out according to the cultural divisions of gender. In a poignant passage in her *Vindication*, Wollstonecraft speaks of having longed for her precursor's 'approbation' when she first conceived of her own work, then mentions her 'sickly qualm' at hearing of Mrs Macaulay's untimely death. (*V*.207)

*   *   *

The connection between women is essential for Mary Wollstonecraft the writer. The feminine bond clarifying, consoling, empowering the struggling self, receives its most intense depiction in *Maria, or The Wrongs of Woman*. The novel is Wollstonecraft's most radical undertaking: she questions the very tenets of truth and rationality she had inherited from the eighteenth-century tradition, setting up at the centre of her narrative a woman incarcerated in a madhouse. The novel opens in this 'mansion of despair'.

Maria struggles to draw her 'scattered thoughts' together
and awakens to a consciousness so passionate, so acute,
a 'whirlwind of rage' that her own sanity seems set at
risk. Memories invade her with 'frightful velocity'. Cries
of despair from the mad fill her with a 'dreadful certainty'.
(MWW.75) What is this 'dreadful certainty'? It is nothing
more or less than a precise knowledge of human passions
pitched to misery, the structure of self reduced to rubble.

'I have rather endeavoured to portray passions than
manners' wrote Wollstonecraft in her Author's Preface,
and the destructive edge of passion becomes crucial to
her evolving theme. (MWW.72) An architectural image
plays into her depiction of the self. When Maria gazes out
of her window at the demented beings who 'strayed along
the walks' she knows she is contemplating 'the most terrific
of ruins – that of a human soul.' Yet the bits and pieces of
architecture that lie in ruin, a broken column or mouldering
archway, however delicately wrought cannot compare with
a ravaged human soul. The mad man or woman is a 'living
memento of the fragility, the instability of reason'. In such
a being, the passions with nowhere to go rush forward
breaking all bounds. They possess a terrible, 'destructive
velocity'. The spectator is overwhelmed by the precarious
nature of human life. There is something 'noxious' in this
untamed profusion, the sheer chaos of passion like some
rich stream overflowing its banks'. (MWW.83)

Yet this by-passing of the normal is crucial to Maria's
survival. She is led to question the arrangements of a world
whose 'civilised depravity' can tear her from her child and
fling her into a mad house. Reason could never have led
her to the radical doubt passion brings. With reason alone,
Maria would have stopped at the despairing, stultifying
insight that the world was 'a vast prison, and women
born slaves'. (MWW.79) Passion, always and irretrievably
sparked off by the concrete particulars of emotive life,
forces her forward. Beyond cruelty and injustice lies the

convulsions of a mind, the brutal disordering of subjectivity that ' . . . like the devastation of an earthquake, throws all the elements of thought and imagination into confusion, makes contemplation giddy, and we fearfully ask on what ground we ourselves stand.' (*MWW*.84)

The radical questioning of self and society that runs through the novel is a function of the madness imaged in it. Shut up in a madhouse Maria is free from the claims of reason as it is socially defined. When a fellow inmate is brought in next door, Maria is breathless listening to the exquisite music that pours from her lips, a 'fair maniac', surely another victim. Yet the next moment garish laughter, and 'a torrent of unconnected exclamations and questions' spill from the singer. (*MWW*.88) The fissures in mentality are disclosed, the gaping wound of madness that haunts a fragile, struggling self. In a 'sublime concentration of thought' the human condition lies revealed. (*MWW*.83) The very anger that drives Maria is what courses through the 'fair maniac', a female other, her senses lost as a result of severe post-partum depression. She had been forced into marriage with a jealous old man, and his treatment of her 'or something which hung on her mind' drew her into madness.

A beautiful crazed woman was described at length in a quotation from *Camilla* by Fanny Burney which Wollstonecraft reviewed in 1796. This 'spectacle of human degradation' was anxiously witnessed by the sisters Eugenia and Camilla.[12] Now with the mad woman holding up a mirror to herself, Maria glimpses the fury of passions that course through her. In his *Madness and Civilization* Michel Foucault points out how passions which stand as the 'meeting ground of body and soul' become the very basis of madness. 'The savage danger of madness,' he writes 'is related to the danger of the passions and to their fatal concatenation.'[13]

In Wordsworth's *Prelude* 'the passions that build up

our human soul' are celebrated, yet the glory of the passions rests on their discipline, their refinement through the action of nature, a procedure in which fear plays a part. (*Prel.*1.7) The convulsion that Vaudracour suffers in Book 9 of *The Prelude*, his mind turned 'imbecile', is a direct result of sexual passion.[14] For Maria, whose fictive existence predates Vaudracour's by six years, the madness to which she (in her sanity) has been condemned is the direct result of her female being, a being corroded by the fatal lack of reason in a world that renders women powerless, reducing the passionate self to a shadow that must survive by existing for men. There can be no sanctity in such discipline.

If in the portrayal of Maria, Wollstonecraft had herself in mind there were other figures, the ruined Marie Antoinette, Marie Roland, even Mary Queen of Scots, who inspired her. Imprisonment as it literally binds in the woman, floods her psychic state with light. The arguments of *Vindication* – of woman as a prisoner of her sex – return in clear episodic fashion.[15]

Directly behind *Maria* stands Wollstonecraft's *Letters*, the writing composed in search of self, the exquisite pain of feeling released and acknowledged. No longer struggling merely against what society deems her to be, the woman nurtures her own instincts of care, her own passion for revelation. The passage is cleared for *Maria* where despair, with all its energy has a didactic edge. Maria's act of writing is literally shaped by the conditions in the prison. Jemima must bring her paper and ink; the wretchedness of the cell, the cries of fellow prisoners assail her. Yet for the first time in her life Maria is free to reflect on her life and tell it in writing. Rejecting the rhapsodies she first scrawled out, she turns to realism and relates the 'events of her past life'. (*MWW*.82) Her longing to address her child, to give her instruction, forces her on, a knife-edge of inspiration sharpened by knowledge only a mother 'schooled in misery' would have the courage to impart. While the conduct books written by men, like Dr Gregory's *Legacy*, told women how to act, their being in the world defined in strict accordance with the claims of propriety, Wollstonecraft's Maria has something more profound.

With the painful authority of a woman who has struggled to live her life, she can cut through the sham of appearances and tell her daughter 'things as they are'. The phrase, which I borrow from Godwin's sub-title to *Caleb Williams* (1794), is relevant to Wollstonecraft's endeavour in *Maria*. Her feminist version of truth telling involves a woman in prison yet one who must still worry through the demands of propriety, have the courage to 'brave censure' and tell her tale. The end, as Maria herself points out in the terrible lucidity that strikes her, is that her child, if alive, might forge for herself a 'grand principle of action'. (*MWW*.124)

The quest for her own voice and with it the capacity to tell and act out the truth, is not enacted in isolation. Female friendship plays a crucial role.[16] Right at the start in her prison cell Maria encounters Jemima, the warder. Her first task is to prove to Jemima that she is actually quite sane. Maria has refused food: 'could anything but madness produce such a disgust for food?' wonders Jemima. (*MWW*.77) Maria's anguish must come to terms with the working-class bluntness of her female companion in prison. Jemima, who has undergone all the degradation poverty and despair could inflict on a woman, seems to her very self a 'monster'. Through her callousness, she once drove a poor pregnant rival to suicide. The 'stiff cold corpse' was discovered in a tub of standing water. (*MWW*.116)

Thrust into the world without love Jemima has gathered rage and cunning. She is brutalised, but survives. This is the candidate for fictive friendship that Wollstonecraft draws into her novel. Without Jemima, Maria could not have kept herself intact. Jemima in turn feels her soul released as she watches the growing love between Maria and Darnford. Jemima then 'voluntarily began an account of herself.' (*MWW*.101) To discover the self, tell it out, leads to truth. The sensibility Wollstonecraft had celebrated in anguished fashion in *Mary*, a fiction where 'the soul of the author is exhibited', blossoms into Romantic awareness. *Maria* is composed of three tales of self that stand as configurations of personal knowledge. The fact that Maria must write her story permits her a permanence, a victory over oppression. At the novel's end it is in writing that Maria must present her case in court. The judge dismisses her plea citing 'the fallacy of letting women plead their feelings'. (*MWW*.198)

As Jemima tells of herself, she reconstructs a severely damaged life. Hearing her, Maria's 'thoughts take a wider range'. She reflects on 'the oppressed state of women' and is filled with sorrow that she has given birth to a daughter. (*MWW*.120) Will the cycle of female degradation continue? Maria is moved to write her life story. Though the memoirs are sent to her lover Darnford, the work is addressed to the new born child torn from her, a being born from her flesh and blood, of whose very existence she is uncertain.

'Always appear what you are', she writes. As 'a mother schooled in misery' she can instruct the child in the very nature of female experience. (*MWW*.124) The madness that might have afflicted her is thrust away. The severance from her child, even as its tragic distance reinstates the meaning of her life, could not have been inscribed and thus worked into meaning without the active intervention of Jemima who at the simplest level furnishes the materials for writing. As a child Jemima had been humiliated by the written word. A cruel step-mother had forced her out shopping with words like 'Glutton, Liar or Thief' inscribed on her forehead. (*MWW*.106) In helping Maria write down her tale, a fragile reparation seems possible for herself.

But what of Darnford, the male figure Maria encounters in prison? How does he enter into the complex and shifting web of the heroine's self-discovery? Right from the very beginning, Darnford as the object of Maria's sexual passion is presented through authorial interventions that stress his shifty, somewhat irresolute nature. Is Maria projecting her long suppressed feelings on to a being ill deserving of them? Her husband Maria writes elsewhere 'would have tortured me, to force me to feel his power . . . ' Wollstonecraft points out quite clearly that the struggle with evil makes her heroine overeager to portray 'the possible virtues the world might contain'. (*MWW*.164) While Pygmalion formed a perfect female body and longed then for an 'informing soul', Maria 'on the contrary, combined all the qualities of a hero's mind, and fate presented a statue in which she might enshrine them.' (*MWW*.99) Is Maria guilty then of succumbing to a 'fatal image'? The phrase is from *Mary* and refers to the sentimental heroines in novels who haunted the young woman's mother, rendering her unfit for the real conditions of female life.

While Maria's benevolent uncle 'my more than father' nurtured her mind, fostering the 'romantic' in her, it is precisely this ideal that misleads her in matters of the heart. (*MWW*.156) She 'falls in love' with George Venables mistaking the reality for the image he presents. 'The romantic turn of my thoughts' Maria realises has betrayed her. She imbues Venables with all the compassion and humanity fit for 'the hero I dubbed.' (*MWW*.130) When she discovers his true character, disgust sets in. Maria's uncle represents benevolent patriarchy. Maria thinks of him as the 'dear parent of my mind'; when he dies, she feels 'widowed'. But the younger men, more overtly objects of desire, present the possibilities of betrayal. Darnford is to Maria what Maria longs for, but is her need too terrible to brook the reality of the man?

When he returns her memoirs to her, he includes a loving letter that recognises her oppression. He resolves to escape with her. Sexual desire opens up the truth of the passions.

Such 'moments of happiness,' writes Wollstonecraft, 'procured by the imagination, may, without a paradox, be reckoned among the solid comforts of life.' (*MWW*.189) But the paradox persists. Desire is knife-edged. Even as it liberates, its very truth may be questioned. While cutting loose a self bound in false reason, desire is still too disturbing to the ordinary world. Darnford, whatever his real self 'was then plastic in her impassioned hand and reflected all the sentiments which animated and warmed her.' (*MWW*.189)

Passion frees and fulfils the female self, yet inspires a terrible uncertainty as to the objects of its knowledge. Even as it liberates the individuated self, it opens up the very grounds of being to question. Hence the convulsion, whose closest visible approximation is madness, striking at the root of self when desire is at its pitch and the old orderings of the world succumb.

Wollstonecraft's creation of a female Romanticism permits her to acknowledge both the ferocity of feeling and the vulnerability of the knowledge founded on it. Uncertainty now becomes part of things as they are. An unknown world is glimpsed at the very borders of the known. Maria, like Dryden's Sigismunda, had 'snapt the chain of theory'. Wollstonecraft's heroine is ready to brave the censure of the world. (*MWW*.86) 'The Heroine' in Dryden's version that Wollstonecraft must have read, 'assum'd the Woman's Place,/confirm'd her Mind, and fortified her Face.'[17] The truth of Sigismunda's desire compelled her to take her stand, empowering her in 'the Woman's Place'. It is a sign of Wollstonecraft's genius that she could subject 'Woman's Place' and with it desire itself to fierce scrutiny, making of her at the very inception of the movement, one of the most powerful of the early English Romantics.

3 Of Mothers and Mamas

John's Language (Dorothy Wordsworth)

On the face of it, the contrast between Mary Wollstonecraft
and Dorothy Wordsworth could not be greater. One thinks
of Wollstonecraft's fierce rebellion against the accepted
codes of her day, contrasting it with the delicate reticence
of her younger contemporary. The call for women's rights
and the public vindication of embattled female existence
would seem distant, even irrelevant to a woman who
lived out her life within the shadow of her brother's
massive genius, her very self a figuration of his vision
of the feminine. Yet to think of Dorothy merely as the
living image of Wordsworth's Lucy ('A violet by a mossy
stone/Half hidden from the eye') would be to miss out on
her genius as a writing woman and her struggle for the
privacy to exist without capitulating to the public realm
and those trammels of propriety that had so troubled Mary
Wollstonecraft.[1]

The paradox of her life, however, is that the privacy
she chose and passion she felt for her brother William
were so intense, absorbing the whole soul of the woman,
that she denied herself a public and autonomous existence
as a writer. Her public silence even as it sheltered her,
could not permit the steadfast development of art, a life's
work whose symbolic power might have eased the pain of
a woman's life.

Yet her brother's patriarchal protection freed her in

early adulthood to discover that 'wonderful prowess in the walking way'.[2] She mapped out her intricate delight in the natural world and its correlate, the realm of the human senses. Dorothy always kept to what was near at hand and directly observable, the actual as it was given to her forming her text, her bodily activity of walking never described in terms of the territorial imperative that underpins Wordsworth's finest meditations. It remained rather a fluid sign that granted her entry into the discrete, refined substances of her perception.[3]

Julia Kristeva speaks of a 'nourishing and maternal' semiotic space in which 'the linguistic sign is not yet articulated as the absence of an object and as the distinction between real and symbolic.'[4] In the perceptual world of Dorothy Wordsworth the absence of a solid subjective centre spells out a proximity to the physical world so acute that language almost retains the function of a rhythmic, presymbolic occasion. This function is brought out clearly in her account of her nephew John's baby sounds.

Looking through her papers in the Grasmere Wordsworth Library, I came across her first Commonplace Book (*DC. MS. 26*). Dorothy's entries open with a note that anchors us in the domesticity of her situation, while signalling the changing family situation in which she found herself. In October 1802 William and Mary Hutchinson were married. The new bride came to Grasmere to live with the brother and sister. The entry in the Commonplace Book dated November 1802 carries us into this world of shared female life starting with an 'Account of Mary's Linen which came from Penrith', a list headed by '2 Hukabak Towels marked J.S'. It includes such disparate items as a 'recipie for making ink' and an ounce of 'Gum arabick'.[5]

In June of the following year, a first child was born to William and Mary and in her Commonplace Book, not long after the details of her sister-in-law's linen, Dorothy includes a fascinating account of her nephew's first sounds. The entry in her hand is headed 'John's Language':

> First inarticulate sounds about 4 months old Googes Googes Gorgen and something like diddle diddle after – Before he was 6 months – Dad Daad – Succeeded by man mam man incessantly – Then dad dad Mam Man. Now 12th March – Man Mam Ma – Dad dad – da pap pap – sometimes – ta ta – often nan, nan nan. Na na, da da nong – (*DC.MS.26.142v*)

The fascination she feels with the baby's first sounds is comprehensible to any one who has been intimately involved with the care of an infant. But Dorothy's entry is not merely an indication of the sorts of attention she lavished on young children. It is her characteristic style to find residence in shared space. Immediately following this first entry on the baby's sounds captured in all the exactitude of any natural occurrence, the murmur of insects, fleeting light, sudden rain, she records the fact that the young child was weaned – more than six months later in actual fact. She links his severance from his mother's breast with first a 'low-spirited' silence and then, after two or three days, an impatient demand for food: 'always with non nan nan nan and something like the German *Nein* – very quick.' The entry continues with John's standing up, roughly a week later, with the help of a stool and his father's wager that he would walk within a week.

While we do not know how soon John walked by himself, the track that is laid down in this Commonplace Book of his earliest development, charts a fluent continuity rather than a rupture. The sounds that he first made, their 'meaning' indistinct, exist in and of themselves. So do the later sounds, though his aunt links them to the demand for food and, as if crossing out any preverbal sense they might have, the German 'Nein'. Still babbling, being weaned, demanding food, then standing up and possibly walking, all co-exist as far as the young child's attention goes within the realm of natural demands and power. The world of symbolic distance, of words that must bridge a gap between the signifier and the signified, is irrelevant.

But isn't this after all just an unself-conscious narrative of a baby's development? Precisely. For Dorothy, the child's first babble, his inclination towards a shadow of speech, his movements and motility, all participate in a realm of undivided being which she celebrated in her own writings. Or perhaps the verb should be *enacted*, for it was in the seeming simplicity of a speech that drew back from the gulf of the overtly symbolic that she sought and found a correlative for her own corporeal identity, one that was quite distinct from the Romantic centralities of perception and naming that her brother consolidated for himself.

Dorothy Wordsworth had earlier expressed a vision of mothering and education when she and her brother set up house at Racedown and took the young Basil Montagu in as a boarder. The child, not quite three, had suffered the death of his mother. Basil, a plant, 'shivering and half-starved', was transformed by six months of the rough and tumble of the Wordsworths' country living into a 'lusty, blooming, fearless boy'.

But what did his education consist of? Almost as if they were true followers of Rousseau's *Émile*, they let the young Basil learn by experience, and from the 'evidence of his senses', the circumambient whole of a maternal nature supplying what mere human agency could never fulfil. In a letter of 1797, Dorothy wrote to her friend Jane Marshall:

We teach him nothing but what he learns from the evidence of his senses. He has an insatiable curiosity which we are always careful to satisfy to the best of our ability. It is directed to everything he sees, the sky, the fields, trees, shrubs, corn, the making of tools . . . He knows his letters but we have not attempted any further step in the path of *book learning*. Our grand study has been to make him *happy*. (*EY*.180)

Wollstonecraft's *Original Stories* (1788)

While the formative powers of joy cannot be underestimated, especially in earliest childhood, it is important to bear in mind that the young Wordsworths relied on the power of a natural setting. And nature of course is pre-given; the values that best fit in with its enjoyment are conservative, preservative, even meditative. For Wollstonecraft in contrast, the world was difficult and dangerous. And far from teaching a child through the evidence of the senses, a notion that assumes a benevolent nature, Wollstonecraft expresses a vision that is sometimes blunt and harsh, working through a pedagogy that presupposes a clear separation between the woman who teaches and the young child who must learn. I am thinking here not about the fluent, meditative writing in her late *Letters from Sweden*, but of the early Wollstonecraft, in particular the stiff didacticism of *Original Stories* (1788).

Wollstonecraft follows here in the eighteenth-century tradition of strict moral instruction for the young. Children's literature, which was a flourishing genre at the time was characterised by an unbending edge of didacticism. Works such as Mrs Barbauld's *Hymns in Prose* (1781) or Mrs Trimmer's *Fabulous Histories* (1786) set up the convention within which the female writer could work. 'Damn them! – I mean the cursed Barbauld Crew', Charles Lamb complained bitterly to Coleridge, celebrating instead a 'beautiful Interest in wild tales'. Children, were trapped into 'knowledge insignificant and vapid as Mrs B's books convey'.[6] The child as a tiny adult, susceptible to evil, requiring firm teaching, was a convention that Blake was to turn so powerfully to his own subversive uses in *The Songs of Innocence and Experience* (1789-94).[7]

In Blake's 'Nurse's Song' from 'The Songs of Innocence' the female guardian finds herself utterly still, poised at the centre of a joyful world. She hears the laughter of the children but it does not disturb, sustaining rather the internal harmony she experiences: 'My heart is at rest within my breast/And everything else is still'. (*B*.15) When she suggests that the children go home to bed, for the sun has set and night dews are visible, the children insist on playing for the birds still fly and sheep still cover the hill. Their logic prevails and the hills echo with laughter. In the contrary poem, the 'Nurse's Song' in 'Songs of Experience', the woman is struck by anxious 'whisperings' – a distortion of the laughter of children. Her own distress consumes her, a wasted past 'fresh' in memory. When she turns to the children she should take care of, her tone is harsh, the bitterness audible in her judgment of them: 'Your spring and your day, are wasted in play/And your winter and night in disguise.' (*B*.23)

Blake, who like Mary Wollstonecraft was part of the circle around the London publisher Joseph Johnson, agreed to provide six plates for Mary Wollstonecraft's *Original Stories*. The first edition was published in 1788, a year of great productivity for Wollstonecraft. In the frontispiece to the illustrated second edition Blake sets the governess Mrs Mason at the foreground of his image. (See plate 2) She is flanked by the two little girls she takes care of. Mrs Mason's didactic function in the work was set out in a subtitle: 'calculated to regulate the affections and form the mind to truth and goodness.'[8]

In Blake's plate, her arms are outstretched over the two little girls, her eyes downcast, either in modesty or to keep up the constant scrutiny of her charges that Wollstonecraft details: she 'never suffered them to be out of her sight' (*OS*.2). Their eyes are raised submissively. The child on the right holds her hands apart; the child on the left crosses them over her breast. Caps ring their heads like haloes. Thrusting the figures into relief is the erect symmetry of doorway and wall, the minute lines of the design filling the grains of wood, the particles of brickwork, the delicate but well trained vines, intrinsic portion of the strict world of human order that Mrs Mason represents. The words used in the frontispiece – 'Look what a fine morning it is. – Insects, Birds, and Animals are all enjoying existence.' – are taken out of Mrs Mason's mouth. It would seem that Blake's image is a satiric comment on Wollstonecraft's governess for the words in the frontispiece are hardly borne out by her own teachings.[9]

Joy has no place in her scheme of things. The two girls are taught the workings of 'cruel necessity' the better to follow the paths of virtue. (OS.v) Their moral education is tinged with cruelty. Indeed Mrs Mason does seem much closer to the harsh nurse of Blake's Experience poem, than to any other quasi-maternal figure.[10] Does Mrs Mason, like that other woman wear a mask, a 'disguise' that has its source in terrible anxiety, perhaps even in sexual repression?

Close to the end of the work Mrs Mason's own psyche is revealed. Casting off from a remark on the 'mutual dependence' ordained by the 'Heavenly Father' – a permission as it were for the introspection that follows – the governess plunges into herself, opening up a subjectivity hitherto concealed: 'I lost a darling child, said Mrs Mason, smothering a sigh, in the depth of winter.' (OS.145) She has suffered a two-fold bereavement, first husband then child. Her terrible isolation discovers an image for itself in the wintry waste that surrounds her, a *paysage état d'âme* consciously set out. The voice quite startling in that it comes from a strait-laced governess, opens up a portion of the female self that was masked over in the stern propriety the didactic role demanded: 'The wintry prospects suiting the temper of my soul, I have sat looking at a wide waste of tractless snow for hours; and heavy sullen fog, that the feeble rays of the sun could not pierce, gave me back an image of my mind.' (*OS*.145-6)

The healing process requires a restoration of Mrs Mason's maternal powers. Since in the work all is fixed and framed in strict accord with didactic needs, Mrs Mason quite shortly after this revelation tells of stumbling on a famished father clutching his infant. The mother is dead, and the father dies shortly thereafter, leaving the child in Mrs Mason's care. Nursing it back to health, she finds her own life quickened, and she is able finally to dispel 'the gloom in which I had been almost lost.' (*OS*.148) With her renewed, if surrogate maternity essential to the young child's survival, Mrs Mason picks up a reason for living again.

In consonance with the impulse to moral propriety that works so powerfully in Wollstonecraft's pre-revolutionary thought, she marks out maternity, a realm identified as the preserve of women, for her particular concern. She draws out the area of possible power: the care and formation of the young. What Simone de Beauvoir was to identify as the fearful 'immanence' to which women are condemned, becomes for this early feminist a matter for careful scrutiny and finally affirmation.[11]

Mrs Mason, the governess, is of course neither a mother nor a home-maker, roles which de Beauvoir identifies as contributing to the peculiar constriction of women. But her status as a woman who once was a mother – her child killed off in tragic if convenient fashion – allows her to stand as the moral centre of a work that requires the theme of a ravaged maternity to link several of its episodes.

In the first chapter, its loose episodic construction typical of the book as a whole, Mrs Mason leads her charges Caroline and Mary into encounters with the life of small animals, a ploy well used by authors of children's books. Yet Wollstonecraft's emphasis is far from the preaching that Mrs Barbauld employs in her *Hymns in Prose*. Her purpose is to teach through example which 'directly addresses the senses, the first inlets to the heart'. (*OS*.iv-v)

In the course of the morning walk, Mrs Mason steps deliberately off a path, tangling her buckle in wet grass. She did this to avoid killing a snail, she explains to Mary. It too was made by God the Father, protector of snails, caterpillars, spiders and children. But startling coda follows: 'You are often troublesome – I am stronger than you – yet I do not kill you.' (*OS*.5) While goodness is the overt subject of the governess's reflections, cruelty underpins its action. Next a soaring lark appears. A nasty boy with a gun shoots down the bird, one of a pair searching out food. This bird, the male, tumbles down, leg broken, wings shattered, eyes thrust out of sockets in 'exquisite pain'. (*OS*.7) Making sure the girls have noticed the creature's suffering, Mrs Mason steps briskly on the tiny neck.

The girls are commanded to pick up the female bird and nurse it. In a brutal world violence seems necessary. The female bird safe in a handkerchief, is borne away together with its young. Now yet another nest must be retrieved, this time from a lad who parts with it for Caroline's sixpence. They had heard the mother bird cry out; its 'intelligible tones of anguish' touched the young girls with 'the emotions of humanity', and they delight in the imagined reunion between mother bird and young. (*OS*.9)

A need to nurture, surely the central impulse of maternal power, has opened up the girls to the quick of feeling and hence the possibility of virtue. The argument seems almost Romantic at this point, the Enlightenment concern with morality mediated through the power of emotion. Further we see an actual woman, acting *in loco parentis*, her example tinged with cruelty considered necessary to quicken the sympathetic imagination of these young girls.

A third example follows closely on. The girls hear the braying of young asses robbed of their mother's milk.

The boy who should have released the mother asses after milking them neglected his duty. Well schooled now, the two girls set free the mother asses then stand and watch in great pleasure as the young ones suck. As in the previous episode the natural principle of maternity is highlighted, placing Mrs Mason's own posture into stark if discrepant visibility. The theological imperative demands a paternal God, creator of the world and all its life, benevolent, instilling order. But in order to convey both the release of feeling and the possibility of human care, Wollstonecraft turns to an unwritten precept one much closer to home, that of maternity. Indeed, it seems to me that a frustrated desire to mother and the contortion of nurture into the need for power underpins Mrs Mason's grim posture, one that Blake might well have wished to satirise.

Of Mothers and Mamas

Contemporary feminists have pondered the realm of maternal care, the rich nurturing capacities that women over the centuries have been entrusted with, the preserving, healing and repairing of the complicated fabric of daily domestic existence, with all the care, labour, tension and ethical choices such a task involves. Adrienne Rich speaks of the 'activity of world-protection, world-preservation, world-repair – the million tiny stitches . . . ' that is woman's particular preserve.[12] Nel Noddings argues for the 'feminine striving for an attainable ideal' as opposed to the will to power and immortality, a 'something beyond'. She contrasts the absolute devotion to a metaphysical ideal represented by the Old Testament patriarch Abraham, with Ceres' search for her missing daughter Proserpine. It is probably in the Old Testament story of the sacrifice of Isaac that the law of the Father, as opposed to concrete, feminine care is most clearly portrayed. In the Greek myth, the grief-stricken mother is still able to turn and care for the boy Triptolemus, who is mortally ill.[13]

Women are capable of all the extremes of violence, savage pain and devotion to perceived absolutes that men are. And it makes a singularly poor argument for feminine virtue, as Mary Wollstonecraft saw so clearly, to claim it necessarily at all times for those who are deprived of power over their own actions. What I wish to illuminate rather, is the way in which women writers often turned away from the abstractions or high sublimity of their male counterparts, to the concrete acts of nurture and care associated with maternity.

Can mothers be replaced? Can the structures of mothering be duplicated? These were questions of critical import to women writers. In an entry in her *Grasmere Journal*, Dorothy Wordsworth describes a visit she paid to Greta Hall where the Coleridges lived. She is accompanied by Mary Hutchinson. The two women come upon Sara Coleridge in the field, then turn indoors, where they encounter the Coleridge children, young Hartley and the baby Derwent. Dorothy reports on the conversation that followed:

> Mary said to Hartley, Shall I take Derwent with me? No says H. I cannot spare my little Brother in the sweetest tone possible and he can't do without his Mama. Well says Mary, why cannot I be his Mama. Can't he have more Mamas than one? No says H. What for? Because they do not love as Mothers do. What is the difference between Mothers and Mamas? Looking at his sleeves, Mothers wear sleeves like this pulling his own tight down and Mamas (pulling them up and making a bustle about his shoulders) so. We parted from them at 4 o'clock . . . Cotton mills lighted up. The first star . . . [14]

Clearly this playful banter is not without deeper import. Hartley's empathic reminder that mothers love uniquely, in a manner that mere mamas cannot, reveals the child's attachment to the formative circumstances of his life. The baby cannot be spared, he would suffer too much at the hands of another maternal care-giver. The natural mother loves in an irreplaceable way. Yet the words 'Mother' and 'Mama' are interchanged with ease in Dorothy's account as the young child's sense of security, poignant in hindsight, firmly rejects the possibility of more than one maternal figure. Still the sense that mothers might be replaced, that mothering might be multiplied through feminine care-givers, emerges in Mary Hutchinson's gentle questions.

Sara Ruddick has reflected on the notion of 'maternal thinking', a feminine stance from which men are not exempt, that couples a careful attention to the concrete needs at hand with a humility to the other. For Ruddick this notion can be translated into a variety of other realms including that of pacifism. She sees the preservative impulse that underlies mothering as standing in direct conflict with militarism, or as in Noddings' analysis, with abstract principles that demand absolute, unquestioning obedience.[15]

For Dorothy Wordsworth the quiet, essentially conservative bent of her nature, sought and found an ethical anchor in the impulse of maternal care. In a short narrative 'Mary Jones and her Pet Lamb' she describes the gradual intertwining of the life of Mary Jones, an only child who lives with her parents, with that of the young, motherless lamb her father brings home one day. Mary Jones fills her waking days with care for the lamb. She feeds it milk, weaves garlands of flowers for its neck and at night dreams about it. The sudden disappearance of the lamb fills the child with grief. She sets out alone across the hills, to search for it. But her joyful recovery of the wandering lamb is framed by fearful loss: 'day light was faded and she could not see her Father's house, or the trees, or the fields.'[16] In this particular narrative, in contrast to *George and Sarah Green*, preservative love and the maternal care that best embodies it clearly win out. Mary's own mother rushes out in search of her daughter and with the help of her husband finally discovers child and lamb fast asleep, Mary's little body warmed by the lamb's coat. The lamb grows into an ewe and bears its own young. The father decides that 'in memory of that night, it should never be killed by knife.' (*DC.MS.121*.8r.)

Susan Levin has argued that 'Dorothy's interest lies in focusing on the enduring, protective relationships between family members and between surrogate mothers and their children, relationships William's work does not favour.'[17] Clearly, in this tale the duplication of maternal care, is critical to survival: the motherless lamb is mothered by Mary Jones who in turn when she is lost, seeking the lamb, is sought out by her own, actual mother. The young girl, out on the cold slopes without shelter is cut from her 'Father's house'. She needs shelter if she is to survive. Time and again in Dorothy Wordsworth's work, a seemingly over-arching power, whether human or natural, must bend to protect and succour the feminine presence.

Masculine Power and the 'Amphibious Life'

A distinction should be made between the kinds of intuitive care and concern that Dorothy occupied herself with, and the didactic vein that Mary Wollstonecraft, Dorothy's great precursor, identified as essential to the tasks of mothering. The clue to the difference can be isolated in the variant perceptions of power. For Mary Wollstonecraft the pedagogic imperative was built into the new woman's existence. In her *Vindication* she imagines a woman, widowed, drawing to herself the androgynous authority, the 'double duty' of both mother and father. (*V*.138) For Dorothy Wordsworth there was no call to retool one's faculties or bear a double burden. In her more meditative, more quiescent vein, she did not think of child rearing as part and parcel of remaking the world. For one thing, the pain of her own early orphancy was too close and what she had, she held on to very tightly. For another, she was not a mother herself, and the burden of caring for children, even as it was detailed and engrossing, did not involve placing herself in the position of a wife. Her concern with child rearing could be set apart to some extent, from the feminist desire to appropriate the pedagogic authority of child rearing.

In the early years of her adulthood Dorothy's place with her brother was cherished, attentively recorded. Topography played its part in her subtle self-definitions. Wollstonecraft's concern with the social, essentially urban definitions of femininity, was quite different from Dorothy's delicate attention to natural landscape. Yet an overlap did exist, the world of women writers in the Romantic epoch defining itself against a feminine self that existed in its phenomenal appearances rather than willed action. At the same time the realms of the domestic and maternal, however ambivalent and shifting, allowed women to claim a rich personal meaning.

In Dorothy's writing, landscapes in their constant mobility, in their fragmented, flickering appearance, permit her to tell of emotions that might otherwise have been repressed. No doubt her extraordinary domestic situation, her give and take in the early years of Alfoxden and Grasmere with her brother William and with their dear friend Coleridge served her well. At times there was a mobility to their shared thought, a vital diffusion of emotion and idea such that the poems and journal entries seem to have burst from one root. At such moments privacy for Dorothy was not solipsism, but a profound sheltering, the act of writing implying its own intimate readers. She had no need then in those early years of her writing life to struggle to reveal the self, to break out of the boundaries of domesticity. Her daily life wove into the tasks of keeping house, the refinements of emotion and image spun from a fabric of thought she shared with her brother.

★   ★   ★

I should stop here to acknowledge a problem that strikes deep when pondering the life and work of Dorothy Wordsworth. Pointing out what was cherished by her in her early writing years, the bond with her brother, the implosive power of scenes struck from daily life and transmuted into her journals, the manner in which life and art seemed to weave together without any visible seams, I have set aside that other Dorothy, the one whose emotions were so repressed that she was forced to throw herself numb on the bed 'neither seeing nor hearing anything', the Dorothy who was clearly terrified of putting herself forward as a poet, feeling she lacked the art, the woman who survived the last two and a half decades of her long life only at the cost of a shattered mentality and fits of depression and violence. (*AGJ*.154)

In a poem entitled 'Power' Adrienne Rich reflects on Marie Curie, her search for the radioactive element causing cataracts in her eyes, skin suppurating on her finger tips, 'her body bombarded for years by the element/she had purified'. Yet to the very end of her life, the poet writes, Marie Curie had to deny 'her wounds came from the same source as her power.'[18] Can one say the same of Dorothy Wordsworth, that her wounds, her repression, her 'madness' even came from the same source as her power? Marie Curie spent her entire adult life dedicated to the cause of a science, her ferocious will, purifying the quest for knowledge. Dorothy Wordsworth never entered the public world, she never 'worked' in that sense, her words, spoken out of desire never entered the currency of literary language except through the consciousness of one or two great poets who were intimate with her writings. Yet it does seem to me that out of the very privacy that sheltered and fostered her genius and granted her power, came the wound, the fearsome isolation, the repression, the hints of instability, which even if they had preceded her adulthood, certainly intensified in the conditions of her public silence.

The contradictions in Dorothy's life are visible in the painful shyness, the 'self-baffled utterance' as De Quincey aptly called it.[19] He notes her intensity, her quickness of demeanour, so frequently noted by others, those 'wild' instincts that thrust her forward into speech and bodily expressivity, only to be checked immediately by her shyness and 'the continual restraint of severe good sense.' (R.199,201) This tension between her own instincts and decorum as she grasped it, between impulse and propriety, is quite far from the idealised portrait that Wordsworth presents in his poetry. De Quincey, sensitised no doubt by his own anguish, was astute enough to glimpse the conflicts within Dorothy, a woman of great creativity, vulnerable though to the gaze of a beloved male other, to the images spun out of his poetic consciousness. Her impulses, bordering on self-conflict seemed to De Quincey almost painful to observe.

In order to reach the power trapped within her own subjectivity, Mary Wollstonecraft, often in ways not wholly raised to consciousness, time and again set up a conflict between patriarchal power (both outside, in the authoritarian structures of society, and internalised within her) and the tumultuous claims of female desire, claims that gathered visibility as she observed the lives of other women. The social world forged a critical dimension of her struggle for a life consonant with the complex, even shattering tension of female desire.

Dorothy Wordsworth's creativity in marked contrast, flourished within the shelter of the natural world, and what in the Grasmere years often seemed like its symbolic extension: her brother William's poetic imagination. Indeed there is a very real sense in which she fostered the passionate interplay between life and poetry that Wordsworth required for the genesis of his greatest art. This meant however that instead of moving into the public world in search of affirmation, Dorothy often ignited her own powers of meaning-making within and through the massive harmonies of her brother's evolving art. The tragic theme of her life then, cannot be wholly severed from the fact that woman in Wordsworth's poetry often occupies a position that is deeply ambivalent, her status as the sometimes obscure object of desire pushing her, in the consciousness of a speaker gripped by the fascination of border states, into an 'amphibious' condition, an in-between position between life and death.

*   *   *

In his drafts and fragments of *The Prelude* (*MS.W.* February 1804) the poet signals his complex pleasure at the sight of a horse that stands on the maternal body of earth, the 'little breast of ground' supporting its weight, stock still in moonlight, mimicking death: 'insensible and still; breath, motion gone,/Hairs, colour, all but shape and substance gone . . . ' Translated through the procedures of the imagination into a creature wholly symbolic, its existence in nature a guarantee of the poet's insight, the little horse by seeming to be dead gathers power over the realm of appearances that haunt the poet. Mimicking death it can enter that kingdom of permanence where desire fuses with its own symbolic meaning. And so without strain or torsion the speaker can describe the creature 'with all his functions silently sealed up,/Like an amphibious work of Nature's hand . . . ' (*Prel.* 498,*MS.W.February 1804*)

Time is struck still in the body of the little horse,

its symbolic power over the constant agitation of human emotions heightened by stillness. It is a stillness it shares with the beloved woman in Wordsworth's 'Lucy' poems where the female figure is either dead or on the brink of vanishing into death, her breath and motion extinguished so that she might all the better stand in for the poet's unutterable desire. 'No motion has she now, no force;/She neither hears nor sees,' the poet had written, turning the dead beloved's weight into the substances of earth, the force of gravity sustaining what is left of her.[20]

While it is possible to argue that the enigmatic Lucy of the 'Lucy' poems stands for the impossible object of poetic desire, the inaccessible meaning that haunts all symbolism, the function of desire as it erases the literal needs to be pondered. In the course of a reflection on the growth of the young child, Jacques Lacan speculates that symbolic utterance could not come into play without activating a 'negativity' to discourse, the disappearance of the Other: 'Thus the symbol manifests itself first of all as the murder of the thing, and this death constitutes in the subject the eternalisation of his desire.'[21]

While the violence, which I am perfectly willing to concede might well be incipient in all poetic knowledge, could work fluently towards Wordsworth's larger aim the refinement of desire, the questioning of 'sense and outward things', for Dorothy, there was no doubt something double-edged in being so seductively drawn in as an object of desire. It is noteworthy that one of the most poignant passages in her *Grasmere Journals* records her numbing pain as William marries Mary Hutchinson, and Dorothy almost unknown to herself records the language of her brother's Lucy poem. In devastating honesty she tells of her own self: 'I could stand it no longer and threw myself on the bed where I lay in stillness, neither hearing nor seeing anything.' (*AGJ*.154)

In marked contrast to this moment of intense, annihilating pain, is the characteristic sensitivity to the details of the natural world that Wordsworth prized in his sister. Yet time and again her feminine powers are set in relief by the claims of masculine genius. In an important passage of *The Prelude*, the speaker insists to his own meditating self-consciousness that the 'prime and vital principle' exists deep within the poet's psyche, cut off necessarily from 'outward fellowship'. The poet moves on to a brief description of the sorts of femininity that might complete and perfect 'the man'. 'Female softness', 'delicate desires' and 'gentlest sympathies' must animate him, even as his heart stands as tender as 'a nursing mother's heart.' (*Prel*.XIII:194,196,207-10)

In the following stanza the poet invokes his sister Dorothy whose 'exquisite regard for common things' restored him to the tenderness and empathy he recognises as essential to a shared human life. (*Prel*.XIII:242) Yet her femininity is clearly most valuable insofar as it exists as a complement to the ever aspiring capabilities of male genius. Addressing her as 'Child of my parents, sister of my soul' he describes how she was able to soften and domesticate his genius. He likens himself to a great, craggy rock, its solitary, sublime strength cut off from the common run of things, dependent on his sister's femininity for a nurture it sorely needs. Her tasks of care and nurture, translated into an extraordinary sort of housekeeping are acknowledged with gratitude as in a potent, discreet act of appropriation, what culture decrees, Wordsworth renders natural.[22]

Of his great rock like being, archetypal image of genius and its aspirations, Wordsworth writes:

> But thou didst plant its crevices with flowers,
> Hang it with shrubs that twinkle in the breeze,
> And teach the little birds to build their nests
> And warble in its chambers. (*Prel*.XIII:234-7)

His desiccation, his 'over-sternness' are softened by the care of his sister, her femininity freely absorbed now into himself, her 'exquisite regard for common things' treasured by his poet's sensibility and enshrined as an intrinsic portion of a healthy creativity. Indeed it is no accident that in the preceding lines Wordsworth had made clear that it was quite precisely his obsessive attachment to what is sublime and terrible, a lesson he has learnt from his canonical master Milton, that his sister had eased for him: 'I too exclusively esteemed that love,/And sought that beauty, which as Milton sings,/Hath terror in it.'

Yet it is equally the case that genius stems from his severe sublimity, rather than her complementary existence for he holds close to himself overt consciousness of poetic power directly 'framed' by nature. The extremities of desire he testified to, even early in childhood ('fostered alike by beauty and by fear') are part and parcel of what Wordsworth thinks of as the estate of poetry, a 'finer knowledge' whose deeply personal nature provides it with an empowering universality. The fact that Wordsworth prized the literal, or 'natural' details of life, arguing at times for the domestic as a public virtue, gathering in, absorbing elements of femininity into his own poetic knowledge, cannot diminish the underlying fact of a gendered world within which his own writing stands. It seems to me that it can only render our reading of Wordsworth more complex, more true, to point out that the centrality of the ego he forged through his astonishing rituals of perception was perfectly in tune with the societal permissions granted the male.

4 Writing in Fragments

'A Collection of Patchwork'

In her 1803 travelogue, *Recollections of a Tour Made in Scotland*, Dorothy Wordsworth describes the tiny, irregular parcels of cottage land as:

> a collection of patchwork, made of pieces as they might have chanced to have been cut by the mantua-maker, only just smoothed to fit each other . . . so small and of such irregular shapes.

She labels her figure 'a woman's illustration'.[1] The image of a patchwork garment, cut of bits and pieces and stitched together as time and resources permit, reflects the realities of a woman's life commonly defined by the hold of the domestic. This stands in contrast to the seamless creation which so often seems to emerge in authorial self-presentation, the claim that the writer's life emerges through his works. Literary labour in such a transaction is rewarded by publication and the overt status it accords the writer, with the private and hidden portion of life transposed through the work into the realm of the public and visible.

In Dorothy Wordsworth's life, however, the privacy that traditionally marked out the female sphere also held sway over her literary productions. Though she wrote copiously, only a tiny portion of what she produced was published in her own lifetime, all within the corpus of her brother's work. These poems like 'Address to a Child', 'The Mother's Return' (*PW*.I.229,230); 'The Cottager to her Infant', 'Loving and Liking' (*PW*.2.51,102); or the haunting 'Floating Island' (*PW*.4.162), were published without her name, marked merely by prefatory tag that identified it as the work of 'my sister' or, as in the case of 'Floating Island' even more cryptically as 'by the Author of Address to the Wind' etc. While Wordsworth seemed quite comfortable including the work of family members in his Poetical Works – 'To a Redbreast' mentioned in the tag to Dorothy's 'Floating Island' is by the 'deceased female Relative' Sarah Hutchinson – Dorothy's own emotions are harder to gauge.

It is as if entry into the public space of authorship, as opposed to the private circulation of her writing, would have disrupted the subtle balance she tried to achieve between her devotion to her brother's genius and other more covert compulsions that moved her as a woman writer. Those compulsions, however, were never tested out in the public sphere in terms of the 'profession of authorship' that De Quincey, her great admirer, felt she ought to have pursued. (*R*.205) In the one case where she came close to publication – at the insistence of the poet Rogers she worked and reworked her *Recollections* in at least five versions of the lengthy text – a publisher was not forthcoming.

Her ambivalence at stepping into the public realm was surely compounded by her choice of genre. In her earlier journals, which contain some of her finest prose, the structure is moulded to the requirements of the private and fragmentary. The domestic sphere of a feminine life interweaves with insights that the most professional of aesthetes might envy. But no hierarchy of imaginative attainment was marked out, no lines drawn between the inner and outer realms.

Elizabeth Hardwick has noted the 'fitful' even 'casual' nature of Dorothy Wordsworth's literary production, arguing that it was inevitable in an 'amateur'.[2] Yet there is a more hidden, more empowering side to her private life that needs to be explored. Within the whole body of her writings, a storm of letters many composed jointly with William, a narrative, the early and late journals, poems, travelogues, with no one genre 'perfected' in the canonically accepted fashion, Dorothy Wordsworth was able to attain a lucidity of language and a quick sensitivity of vision that an overtly symbolic undertaking might well have engulfed.

Writing without any place readily accorded her in the public world, indeed relinquishing the possibility of such a place for her feminine self, she was able to exploit her enforced marginality and embrace the form of the fragment. To speak of the private and fragmented in her female life and letters means facing up to some of the more intimate processes of her thought, both how she grasped herself as a writer, and how that grasp of self was moulded by her day to day situation in her brother's household. The domestic details of her ordinary life, the chores of cooking and cleaning house, washing, ironing, baking, digging in the garden, 'sticking' peas are juxtaposed with notations of working with her William on his poems, copying them out, listening to him recite them. They are juxtaposed too with those delicate descriptions of nature so highly prized by Wordsworth and Coleridge in which Dorothy, closely bound to each of the poets, sets out her sense of reality, the ordinary objects of perception, grass, insects, tree trunks, clouds, skirmishing, even as they enter her consciousness, with an almost visionary edge to perception.

Yet her figure is curiously elusive, life seeming to overwhelm her writing, the latter splintered through the pressures of domestic living. Then there are the problems posed for a reader by the tragic 'posthumous life' of her last two and a half decades.[3] Her days were eked out in a bed-chamber, or in a wheelchair at Allan Bank. In a letter of 1838 she describes her thoughts as a 'wilderness'. And her brother mourned her darkened existence: 'My dear Sister . . . her mind . . . much shattered. The change . . . probably was preparing before.'[4]

The 'madness' Dorothy suffered from, whatever the clinical causes, was quite real, a dark, backward opening into her earlier emotional difficulties, the palpable insecurities of the *Grasmere Journal*, pierced though at the time by a luminous near visionary bliss. The great walker, the woman who had rejoiced in her power and freedom to walk abroad, was condemned to a stifling immobility. We are left the fragments of text she composed in the last years, journals inscribed in a hand that grew more illegible as her condition worsened, scraps of letters, whole drafts of poems suffused with nostalgia.

It is not known what Dorothy Wordsworth thought of Mary Wollstonecraft. In a journal entry for April 14, 1798 she cryptically notes the arrival of the posthumous *Memoirs* that Godwin composed to honour his wife. Their candid account of Wollstonecraft's struggles with propriety and the revelation of her love affairs was to cause a backlash against the author of the *Vindication*. Dorothy, who no doubt was aware of her brother's disillusionment with Godwinian rationalism, wholly inadequate a basis it seemed to him for social justice and the intimate self, says nothing about her own response to Godwin's picture of his dead wife. The entry is brief, and the sentence 'Mary Wollstonecraft's life, etc., came,' is prefaced by notations of walking in the woods, then staying indoors because of a stormy evening. (*AGJ*.13) No further comment is offered. One is left to imagine Dorothy's feelings on reading the *Memoirs*. An admirer of Richardson's *Clarissa* in her younger days, she must have responded to the genuine feelings that irradiated Wollstonecraft's life.

The breakdown of Dorothy's last years suggests a basis

for comparison with Wollstonecraft's own preoccupations
at the very end of her life. In terms of a woman's life-cycle,
however, there was no parity. Wollstonecraft's life was cut
short when she was merely thirty-eight years old. Dorothy
Wordsworth lived on till a month after her eighty-third
birthday. Maria, heroine of Wollstonecraft's last novel is
flung into an asylum. But Maria is not mad. It is precisely
because her female sanity is defined as 'mad' by a conniving
world that the woman robbed of her rights, finds herself
incarcerated. The prison, fit replica of the constraints of
a culture most unnatural where women's freedoms are
concerned, both entombs her and sets her free, the mind
cut loose of its shackles, the torments of daily life forcing
her forwards till she questions the very basis of ordinary
existence. In Dorothy Wordsworth's case, the breakdown
of sanity is no metaphor. It is a literal rendering of what
tragically befell her in the last two decades of her life. The
temptation to read the end of her life as entirely symbolic
of the female condition must be avoided. Yet the splintered
testaments of those last years can be linked with both clarity
and compassion to earlier expressions of her articulate self,
illuminating something of the hidden, even bruised links
that ingather the creative psyche to a female life.

Orphancy and Shelter

A fear of displacement, even a sense of being unhoused
are visible in Dorothy from the earliest years in which
we have news of her. Born on Christmas Day, 1771, she
was profoundly marked by the tragic death of her mother
Anne. The little girl just six, was parted from her four
brothers and father and sent to live first at Halifax with
her Aunt Elizabeth Threlkeld, a fine upstanding woman
who educated the growing girl as best she could. The pain
of a family 'squandered abroad' struck her most forcibly

when she was sent away as a teenager from Halifax where she had been relatively happy, to lodge at Penrith with her maternal grandparents. (*EY*.15)

From Penrith, in 1787, Dorothy opened out her heart in a series of letters to a close friend from Halifax, Jane Pollard. The friendship with Jane, a girl her own age and daughter of a local mill-owner, served Dorothy well.

Female friendship was a haven for her restless intelligence, for those complex feelings the social world would have censured. Indeed the early letters to Jane Pollard serve much the same function in Dorothy's young life, as the letters Wollstonecraft wrote as a young adolescent to her friend Jane Arden. In each case the epistolary bond provides the writer with a way of laying bare her emotions, sorting out her place in the world, a task that otherwise might have seemed impossible. At fourteen Wollstonecraft wrote of such female friendship: 'Its pleasures are permanent and increase by reflection, so that a view of the past adds to the enjoyment of the present, opening to the mind the prospect of endless bliss.' (*WL*.62)

The bond with Jane Pollard, later Jane Marshall was to remain with Dorothy all through her life. In a later poem inscribed in her Commonplace Book and entitled 'Irregular Verses' she spells out the intense bonding of these two young women, their early prospects of 'endless bliss', as well as their season of thwarted wishes.[5] The dream of a shared dwelling emerges with great clarity in this poem. 'Hope untamed' has led the poet to a magical dream cottage. Decked with all the furniture of fantasy, it masks the dreariness of an ordinary world over which two young women have little power:

> A cottage in a verdant dell,
> A foaming stream, a crystal Well,
> A garden stored with fruit and flowers . . .
> And sheltering all this faery ground,

A belt of hills must wrap it round,
Not stern or mountainous, or bare . . .

The cottage risen up from desire is well stocked, well girded, reflecting to perfection the feminine need for a fruitful and sheltered domesticity. A bountiful nature can grant what in the ordinary world would require the intervention of patriarchal power. Yet this 'faery ground' existing within the mind's own space dwindles away precisely because of a lack of support from external reality. The onset of the adult world of decorum and duty compels the young women to part and Dorothy records how the dream of a shared cottage dissolves into the baseless fabric of longing: 'Alas! the cottage fled in air,/The streamlet never flowed . . . ' Jane gains dignity, lives out a life of 'usefulness', marrying, giving birth to children.

While leaving her own past in the shadows, Dorothy turns to the problem of writing poetry. She imagines Julia Marshall, Jane's daughter, the listener of the poem, asking her why she had not earlier turned to the poetic enterprise, if only to set down 'pleasant guileless dreams'. The query is couched in the language of ironic self-diminishment. For it is not high art of the bard, firmly ensconced in the tradition of Milton to which she refers. Rather the woman writer alludes to the 'jingling rhyme' of her creation, an entirely lower form of expression.

Yet self-diminishment cannot entirely protect her from the memory of poetic ambitions. 'The tender Lays/Of them who sang in Nature's praise' she writes, her very phrase recasting her own earlier desire which 'reverenced the Poet's skill,/And might have nursed a mounting Will'. The analysis of failure is set out, a sobering correlative to the merely dream existence of the dwelling place. A crushing lack of self-confidence emerges as the cause of her silence, with its symptoms of 'bashfulness', 'struggling shame' fear of blame by elders, or ridicule from peers. Even the 'mild maternal smile' that might have helped, is interpreted as reproof. The self unable to search out external pathways for its expressivity is now trapped by 'lurking pride' and 'a fond self-love'.[6] It is as if the composition of poetry, as opposed to the finely textured prose style she perfected for herself, brought Dorothy Wordsworth into conflict with an outer standard of accomplishment, one that was revealed most powerfully for her in her brother William's acts of creativity.

In a letter of 1804, Dorothy paints a vivid picture of William striding back and forth in the rain, oblivious to the outer weather. His concern with the inner world of poetry is so intense, she notes, that he might even be 'fast bound within the chosen limits as if by prison walls'. Meanwhile she is indoors. It's been a busy time in the household. It's May and 'fitting beds and curtains', the labours of 'Whitsuntide cleaning, colouring and painting' have hardly left her time to sit and reflect, set pen to paper in 'the quiet possession of myself and my own thoughts.' (EY.476,477)

The figure of the male poet intensely self-absorbed, composing as he walks is etched into her mind. In 1806 she writes again to Lady Beaumont, bringing up her own attempts to compose as she walks. The context for the comparison is established early. Dorothy thanks her friend for praising two of her poems, which William had recited aloud while on a visit to the Beaumonts. Disclaiming any credit for her productions, she sets down 'the history of those two little things which William in his fondness read to you'. The first poem 'Address to the Wind' came to her while writing a letter to William and Mary. Thinking of her little nephew Johnny, and 'having paper before me', she wrote down the lines 'and went on till I had finished'. She adds that the other poem, probably 'The Cottager to her Infant', was composed in similar fashion. The deliberate, self-conscious act of composition is firmly set aside. Dorothy adds she could never write for adults, only for children. The familiar disclaimer based on gender takes on an added poignancy as the writer of the *Alfoxden and Grasmere Journals* admits: 'but I have no command of language, no power of expressing my ideas . . . ' One must clarify, however, that she is talking about 'language and numbers', metrical composition and implicitly all that it involves by way of tradition and accomplishment. Her own peculiar model, that of her brother ill suits her. Try as she might, she cannot step into William's footprints:

> I have often tried when I have been walking alone (muttering to myself as is my Brother's custom) to express my feelings in verse; feelings, and ideas such as they were, I have never wanted at those times; but prose and rhyme and blank verse were jumbled together and nothing ever came of it.[7]

Language in its set form betrays her. The script of a reified tongue splinters into bits. Her incoherence strikes her, contrasting forcefully with her brother's example, his fluency impossible for her to attain. Not surprisingly, it was when she was freed from the constraints of set forms that she wrote at her finest, the fears that struck so close to home – a direct concomitant of her female gender – erased. And if such erasure required the emptying out of the self, that was not too high a price to pay for the precise visions of the *Alfoxden and Grasmere Journals*.

It is possible to see in her early orphancy the roots of this authorial predicament. Painfully struck by the lack of a 'father and a home', the adolescent Dorothy in 1787 recoiled into herself, longing for the supportive love that she was robbed of. There was no temptation for her in the public existence the young Wollstonecraft struggled towards, the family of origin left behind, others sought out who could help her achieve her own independent goals. For Dorothy

Wordsworth the ideal of supportive love was to meld with the notion of family, lost and then reconstituted in early adulthood.

In a letter of March 1805, composed after the death of her brother John, she tells of 'fraternal affection' that has filled the earlier void. Such love seems to her to be 'the building up of my being, the light of my path'. The twinned images of a building or dwelling and a path are not inimical to each other. As the self is built up through love, that same love foretells the future, drawing out the track of a shared source. A mother's caring stolen by death must be recollected as best possible. 'Our Mother, blessed be her Memory, was taken from us when I was only six years old. From her I know that I received much good that I can trace back to her.' (*EY*.473)

We see how her voice defines the self through an intimate mesh of connection. Employing the image of the self as a structure or building, William Wordsworth in *The Prelude* evokes the death of his mother:

> The props of my affection were removed,
> And yet the building stood, as if sustained
> By its own spirit. (*Prel*.II.294–6)

The self is 'left alone' but fed and sustained by a visible world which seems capable of filling up the terrible void of maternal loss. Later, in the same book of *The Prelude* the poet refers to his poem, based on the stuff of autobiography, an 'interminable building reared/By observation of affinities/In objects where no brotherhood exists/To common minds . . . ' (*Prel*.II:402-5) The disparate details of the visible world are forged by the poet's imagination into a vast structure, fit dwelling for his genius. The architectonics of the mind in action become central to the validity of poetic skills. The power of the poet's eye makes the midnight storm grow darker.

The visible world, however, has a very different status in Dorothy's finest writings. It gathers powers and luminosity precisely to the extent to which it is shorn of the overt hold of the self. For her the literal is distanced from the turbulence of imaginative need and turns mystical in its lack, in the subtraction from it of the mind's hold. And so for Dorothy Wordsworth, in contrast to her brother William, the image of a building or shelter, a trope for the self, comes often to stand for an actual dwelling, not a textual one, a shelter that is shared with a loved other. Gender would seem crucial, the woman's sense of self intrinsically bound up with the lives of others, rather than developed in exclusion from them. A striking correlative to such a sense of self is that the powerful counter-world of symbolism is then cast aside in favour of the actual.

At a moment of intensity in the *Grasmere Journals*, in the course of a reflection on moonlight that illuminates hills and lake water, Dorothy flirts with the symbol-making powers she senses are crucial to poetry. And the literal building she sees on the island, rises up as a trope for the self. In the entry for Thursday, March 18, 1802 she writes: 'I had many very exquisite feelings and when I saw this lowly Building in the waters among the Dark and lofty hills, with that bright soft light upon it, it made me more than half a poet.' (*AGJ*.104) But on returning home exhaustion strikes her, she gives up trying 'to write verses'. She cannot take heart from the separate self required for poetry. The diffused flexibility of prose, where things as they are given are raised to visibility, suits her better. The building on the island, however 'lowly' cannot stand up of its own accord; the circumambient landscape must both encircle and support it.

Images of the cottage or shared dwelling, expressions of the persistent desire to be housed, as opposed to constructing a home in the world, are sprinkled throughout the earliest letters. The first sharer is the female friend

Jane. Dorothy, as an adolescent longing for a sister, laughs at her skill as an 'architect' of castles in the air. But this make believe Castle or Tower of Joy' as she later dubs it, gives way a few years later to the more substantial dream of a 'little Parsonage' to be shared with her brother William. (*EY*.12,84,90) This second image was formed in February 1793 when Dorothy was twenty-one. She writes of 'the chain that links me to my Brothers', which 'neither absence nor Distance nor time can ever break'. Within its adamantine links, the young woman sought a harbour for herself. Even a blissful domesticity seemed entirely possible.

Fantasies sometimes take forms that are socially sanctioned. Discovering in her brother William's genius fit company for herself, Dorothy decks out her desire in the furniture of a conventional bliss. The requirements of 'notability' that so irked her in her grandmother can be safely cast aside, and neither 'Ridicule' nor 'Censure', two modes of societal denial so crushing to a sensitive young woman, will hold sway. The shared life with William would release a finer self that the common round might crush. Now the seasons of the year, far from engulfing the writer will flow smoothly, each in concord with a 'particular scheme of happiness':

> When I think of winter I hasten to furnish our little Parlour, I close the Shutters, set out the Tea-table, brighten the Fire. When our Refreshment is ended I produce our Work, and William brings his book to our Table and contributes at once to our instruction and amusement, and at intervals we lay aside the Book and each hazard our observations upon what has been read without the fear of Ridicule or Censure. (*EY*.84)

Reading these letters in full knowledge of her later passionate bond with William, it seems inevitable that as the social conventions of the day drew her from the intimacy of female friendship, Dorothy should turn to her brother, her feelings for him cemented through the ferocity of a childhood love, lost and reclaimed in adulthood. 'I am very sure,' she wrote in a letter to Jane Pollard 'that love will never bind me closer to any human being than friendship binds me to you my earliest female friend, and to William, my earliest and dearest male friend.' (*EY*.92-3) If such intensity meant that she was 'heretical' in her 'opinions concerning Love and Friendship', it was a risk she was willing to accept.

Yet the house with William, which finally became a reality for Dorothy in the whitewashed, neat boned frame of Dove Cottage, had at times been a precarious dream. In a letter of February 1793 she tells Jane not to ignore the 'dark and broad Gulph' that still separates her from the 'little gilded Cottage'. The adjectives used to describe the gulph echo quite precisely those William uses in his poem addressed to Dorothy, 'An Evening Walk' where he writes: 'For dark and broad the gulph of time between/Gilding that cottage with her fondest ray . . . ' (*PW*.I.36-68) But by June of that year Dorothy learned of the affair with Annette Vallon. The dark reality of the sexual world ripped the fabric of dream. All now seemed 'obscure and dark' to Dorothy. No longer able to 'foresee the day of my felicity', she held fast to her love for Jane for solace. (*EY*.86,89)

Indeed unhousedness most forcefully manifest when love, and the security it represented were threatened, haunts much of Dorothy Wordsworth's early life. At times the terror that comes upon her results in a fragmentation, a critical inability to compose herself, to make the bits and pieces of the real world hold together. We see this in a letter composed in 1787 at the age of fifteen. First her wit and intelligence strike the reader, her restless humour at the expense of her grandmother, of whom the writer notes: 'There is not one person who is a favourite with her that I do not dislike'. (*EY*.9)

Instructing her ceaselessly on the proper notions of decorum, her grandmother had set Dorothy to work, sewing and mending. But the girl was secure enough in her sense of self to wake up very early to read and write, her interests in fashions of the day, high heels and curled hair underpinned by more serious, more sustaining concerns. The letters contain an elaborate list of the reading materials her brothers provided her, the catalogue running through Homer's *Iliad* and *Odyssey*, a promise of Shakespeare's plays, Milton, Hayley, Fielding, *Gil Blas* by Alain-René Lesage, as well as the notorious work which caused Mary Wollstonecraft so much grief, 'Gregory's Legacy to his Daughters'. (*EY*.7-8)

While the act of writing to her friend Jane has allowed Dorothy to lay out portions of her fifteen-year-old existence and so compose herself, the opening paragraph with its hints of irreparable terror cannot be forgotten. She cannot 'paint', she says, her distress at parting from her brothers: 'for a few hours I was absolutely miserable, a thousand tormenting fears rushed on me, the approaching winter, the ill-nature of my Grandfather and Uncle Chris . . . ' The items in 'quick succession' fill her mind, the fragments jolting, displacing the more settled self she longs for. 'Could I write to you', asks Dorothy plaintively 'while I was in this situation?' (*EY*.5)

Writing and Walking

Writing requires a calmer self, a better self whose poise is untouched by a turbulent and fragmenting emotion. In order to reach that self, the excesses of feeling and desire have to be set aside. Even as she recognised the undertow of a passionate insecurity, Dorothy Wordsworth in some of her most powerful writing constructs a series of strategies, both biographical and textual, to escape it. The opening of the *Grasmere Journals* offers a vivid instance. In the entry for May 14, 1800, the writer points to a critical self-division, a cleft in her thinking and feeling being that the act of writing both springs from and must suppress. This double, conflicting task for the psyche stems from a 'quarrel' within herself. (*AGJ*.15)

As William leaves Dove Cottage to set off for Yorkshire to meet Mary Hutchinson, Dorothy who has shared his most intimate literary life, reading, editing, transcribing his poetry, indeed helping create the stuff out of which that poetry is spun, feels enormously desolate. She sits overwhelmed on a stone by Grasmere lake, tears welling up in her. Weeping serves to ease her, yet she cannot absorb the lake into her own intensity, the 'pathetic fallacy' as Ruskin was to call it, illusory to a woman whose lucidity when it came to the visible world, had few equals.[8] The lake is left to its own 'heavy sound' which she will not or cannot connect to her own torment: 'The lake looked to me *I knew not why* dull and melancholy . . . ' (*AGJ*.15, my italics) Her transparency serves her well. With her own deepest feelings doubled within, the landscape outside stands preserved in all its singular loveliness. As she walks, seeking an exit from her own overwhelming self, she finds release in the minutiae picked out by her eye.

> A beautiful yellow, palish yellow flower, that looked thick and round and double, and smelt very sweet – I supposed it was a ranunculus – Crowfoot, the grassy-leaved Rabbit-toothed white flower, strawberries, geranium – scentless violet, anemones two kinds, orchises, primroses. The heckberry very beautiful, the crab coming out as a low shrub. (*AGJ*.15)

These fragments of perception named in a slow, resolute catalogue, set out shards of an earthly paradise she has done nothing to create. The flowers invade and console the keeper of the journal. The precision of naming creates its own decorum, breaking suddenly at a detail almost erotic in its starkness: 'Met a blind man driving a very large beautiful bull and a cow.' Her brief narrative continues. She enters Dove Cottage, the home in which she is now all alone and sits down to write. The cold cannot deter her. She explains her reason for writing. Her fragile yet potent sensibility struggles with a fierce unrequited power, a passion which can consume. The act of writing must hold her together as she endures this 'quarrel'. She must keep a journal, a record of her days till her brother's return. 'I set about keeping my resolve because I will not quarrel with myself, and because I shall give Wm. Pleasure by it when he comes home again.' (*AGJ*.15-16)

If sometimes out of the quarrel with ourselves we make poetry, there are other times that such a quarrel might splinter a self all too delicately constituted. The evasion here, it seems to me, is not of the self, as some critics have suggested, but rather of contorting passion that might destroy the boundaries of a female life delimited with great care. The self is identified with more than mere intensity of feeling. This is no longer the realm of young Werther, nor of a Mary Wollstonecraft who twice attempted suicide in 1795, both times in her despair at her lover Imlay's infidelity. The second time, not content with an overdose of laudanum she pitched herself off Putney bridge but was rescued by a boatman. In clear contrast, Dorothy in her adulthood chose the path of containment and a feminine self that would be responsible for the lives of others. Her place in the shared world was at stake.

Hence the hold of the domestic, the practical labour women were born to, which she treasured in her early years almost as a ritual ordering of the day to day life; hence the fragments of her journals where she resolutely bypasses any attempt to explain her inner feelings. Instead, the brilliant shards of a perceived world mark out the shifts of her mood, the transitions spelt out in terms of the changeable light or weather or those shifting sounds to which she was acutely sensitive. And so she will write in an entry for January 23, 1798 of 'the absence of the singing of birds, the hum of insects, that noiseless noise which lives in the summer air.' (*AGJ*.2) Or on March 1st of the same year she notes the mist that passes over sheep, its vaporous forms seeming 'to have more of life than those quiet creatures'. A cryptic phrase follows: 'The unseen birds singing in the mist.' (*AGJ*.9)

The senses, far from being baffled by the distinctly intangible, corroborate each other, gathered into a flowing unity, an ebb and flow of sensorial power that often characterises her entries. If the sheep are unheard, the birds are unseen and the failure of sight here simply betokens the depth and persistence of the natural world into which the female writer is plunged. The emphasis is subtly removed from the self and cast on to the objects of perception, however shadowy they may seem. Here is a humility in the face of the perceptible world, opposed to the intense self-awareness that Keats was to identify as the governing stance of the 'Wordsworthian or egotistical sublime; which is a thing per se and stands alone'. While he recognised Wordsworth as setting his poetic self over and against the perceived world, Keats favoured his own style of consciousness, one that could thrive through the imaginative dissolution of ego, entering empathetically into 'some other Body', a man, a woman, a room full of children, a sparrow pecking on the sill.

Yet one must be cautious here in turning back to Dorothy's own literary strategies. To draw her into the mesh, however delicate, of what Keats termed 'Negative Capability' would be to miss out on her scrupulous adherence to the literal, a devotion that did not permit her to indulge either in the intensity that welled up within her, or in speculations as to the metaphysical status of that 'more than natural loveliness' she was often acutely aware of. (*K*.193,386-7)

* * *

Dorothy Wordsworth was a great walker. In company with her brother, Coleridge, or by herself she strode about the hillsides of Alfoxden and Grasmere. From Alfoxden she wrote in delight to Mary Hutchinson: 'The hills that cradle these valleys are either covered with fern and bilberries, or oak woods, which are cut for charcoal . . . Walks extend for miles over the hill-tops . . . ' (*EY*.171) Of the often brief entries for the five months recorded in the *Alfoxden Journal*, January to May 1798, at least fifty-two begin with the verb 'Walked' or some variant 'Went', 'Set forward' or 'Turned'. At times the entries lack a subject, the verb seems ample. Once in the notation for March 31st, the verb stands stark, quite isolate, 'Walked', as if the burden of meaning could be borne by it, the task of mobility preserved. But the isolate verb is embedded in a series of cryptic entries, as if bodily mobility were charged with opening up the text for her: 'Walked I know not where'; 'Walked'; 'Walked by moonlight'. The two prior entries 'Hung out linen' and 'Coleridge dined with us' had already gripped the writer's tiny reckonings of experience to the daily round.

Yet the activity of walking is just one facet, if the most palpable one, of a fascination with mobility that drew her into the very process of the natural world, both her seeing eye and the world that entered into visibility haunted by movement and change. Coleridge's acute sense of Dorothy – 'her eye watchful in minutest observation of nature; and her taste a – perfect electrometer' – seems drawn at least in part from her concern with natural process.[9] 'All the Heavens seemed in one perpetual motion when the rain ceased', she notes in the *Alfoxden Journal*, alerting us to the constancies of an inconstant weather, where light, water and cloud could part and reform, affording ceaseless delight to the eye. Later in the same month she notes the surface of the heath – 'restless and glittering with the motion of the scatterd piles of withered grass, and the waving of the spiders' threads.' The same day, looking down now from a hill top, she notes 'miles of grass, light and glittering, and the insects passing.' (*AGJ*.4,6)

Yet the 'perpetual motion' she notes again, two days later, this time in relation to the damp adder's tongue and fern in the valley below is never drawn back into a tight centre of vision. Though the observer's position or 'station' is often given, in accordance with the conventions of the picturesque gaze, the world's flux is never knotted aback into the hold of self-consciousness. The concern with beauty, curiously for one writing in the Romantic epoch, is freed of the self's centrality. The contrast with William Wordsworth can clarify this point. In the first book of *The Prelude* when the adult voice seeks to convey that 'unconscious intercourse' the small boy held with 'eternal beauty' we glimpse the motion of light, as it is ingathered by the child's eye. The child stands still at the water's edge:

> Even while mine eye has moved o'er three long
>   leagues
> Of shining water, gathering as it seemed,
> Through every hair-breadth in that field of light
> New pleasure, like a bee among the flowers.
>   (*Prel*.I:605-8)

The earthly paradise, visible in the expanse of light that stretches over the ocean, even as it stands as an emblem of natural divinity, serves to illustrate the quickening imagination of the young boy, parent as it were, to the troubled, questing adult.

In the journals of Dorothy Wordsworth, there is no such overt symbolic procedure. The mind's task of meaning-making is not imaged overtly in visual activity. Rather it is as if the very quick of consciousness were displaced on to the mobility glimpsed in the natural world. And such displacement can work its way into her more carefully elaborated landscapes, such that in hindsight it is possible to grasp in the bodily activity of walking, an iconic representation of a motion that underpins the external world. In the opening entry to the *Alfoxden Journal* she sets out a description of the 'paths' and 'channels' made by running water. The water cuts through the hillside vitalising it, joining the discrete elements of vision. It runs down the ridges, streaks the young wheat, thrusts bodies of sheep into relief. Then sunbeams take over the lively task. Light is fertile to the gaze, it 'peoples' the countryside. The eye focuses on the details of early spring flowers, hepatica and snowdrops, moving in conclusion to the 'slanting woods of an unvarying brown' that lead back up the hillside, the ridge covered with tree shafts that seem 'columns of a ruin'. (*AGJ*.1) The image draws out the fragmentary nature of the depicted whole, inevitable when the writer struggles to convey a ceaseless process.

Consciousness, far from emanating and returning to a central self whose acts of vision illuminate the landscape, discovers itself as displaced, lacking a durable place in which to be. Indeed this displacement becomes an aspect of the flux she celebrates and is rarely far from the surface of perceptual knowledge.

Such an abnegation of the central hold of subjectivity stands in contrast to the earlier developing Romanticism of her predecessor, Mary Wollstonecraft. In her first fiction, *Mary*, Wollstonecraft describes the elsewhere the young woman was forced to seek for herself – at first a bleak, minimal shelter in the womb of nature, sufficient to her needs, 'the cavity of a rock covered with a thin layer of earth'. (*MWW*.9) Shorn of parental love, the growing girl curls up in the cave and reads voraciously, feeding her hungry mind: Milton's *Paradise Lost*, Thomson's *Seasons*, Young's *Night Thoughts*. In *Night Thoughts* one imagines her coming across these lines she might well have marked and pondered:

> Gold is poor
> India's insolvent: Seek it in thyself,
> Seek it in thy naked self, and find it there . . . [10]

In the quest for a true treasure the spirit renounces gold and diamonds. India, the mythic hinterland is cast aside. Consciousness must plunge into itself. Struggling to enter her 'naked self' Mary lives out a life filled with tormenting contradictions, yet she survives, mutilated but intensely self-conscious, composing fragments touched with an agonised sublimity.

Dorothy was sixteen in 1788, the year *Mary* was published, and she might well have read the novel, though no account of such a reading remains. One wonders what she would have made of that fictive life, her own marking out a radically divergent path. Even as she sought out a new, uncharted life for herself, Dorothy in the strategies of her writing pulled away from the 'naked self', away as best she could from the torments of consciousness. The new realm she sought was constantly in motion, created and recreated by the nameless natural powers that surround the self. The sheer delight of such a force is manifested in the restless compositions she sought out for her eye, correlates as it were for the mind's activity. In a passage in her *Recollections* (1803) she tells of a scene by Dumbarton Rock where the constant motion of the elements creates:

> a new world in its great permanent outline and compo-
> sition, and changing at every moment in every part of
> it by the effect of sun and wind, and mist and shower
> and cloud, and the blending lights and deep shades

which took the place of each other, transversing the lake in every direction. The whole was indeed a strange mixture of soothing and restless images . . . yet intricate and homeless, that is, without lasting abiding-place for the mind . . . (*JDW*.253)

The last phrase is telling. The homeless female mind finds its most potent images, not in the firmness of a dwelling place made with hands, but in the flux that underlies all of existence, the inhuman world drawn in as witness to the earthly predicament. Orphancy has been transmuted to this spiritual and aesthetic pleasure, discovering in what is given to eye and ear, sources of perpetual changefulness. The poignancy of such knowledge, however, cannot be lost sight of. Loss underpins it, and the fragment must stand as its surest formalisation.

5 Natural Enclosures

Of Passion and Place

In 1795 Mary Wollstonecraft visited Altona in the course of her Northern travels. Three years later, Dorothy Wordsworth came to the same place, accompanied by her brother and Coleridge. Virgina Woolf notes in an essay on Dorothy the sharp divergence between what these 'two highly incongruous travellers' saw. Wollstonecraft, who 'dashed her head against wall after wall' in torment, struggling to decipher her imperishable part, 'this I so much alive', stands out in vivid relief against Dorothy Wordsworth, whose subtle notations of what she actually saw do little to dramatise her own part in the seeing of things, her own 'I'. Woolf comments that in the case of the younger woman, her ' " I so much alive" was ruthlessly subordinated to the trees and the grass'.[1]

This repression of self is linked to Dorothy's obsessive need to be absorbed into the tasks of caring for, indeed *being* for her brother. 'She gave me eyes, she gave me ears', Wordsworth wrote in 'The Sparrow's Nest', but such gifts while acknowledged were underwritten by the almost boundless devotion that led Dorothy to more than merely literary labours for him. (*PW*.1:227) Her acts of reading and writing for him, keeping journals which set the first drafts for numerous lyrics, her careful, persistent editing of his works, were all subsumed in the resolute passion that marked her bond with William. 'After dinner we made a pillow of my shoulder, I read to him and my Beloved slept . . . ' she notes in the *Grasmere Journal* in the entry for Wednesday March 17,1802. (*AGJ*.102-3) Later in the evening, walking by the side of Rydale Lake, Dorothy is struck by a red light on Silver How. It seems to her to rise from the valley below. She quotes lines which might have come from a draft of Wordsworth's *Peter Bell*:

> There was a light of most strange birth
> A Light that came out of the earth
> And spread along the dark hill-side. (*AGJ*.103)

The mysterious light makes the hillside visible and she sees 'the shape of my Beloved in the Road at a little distance'. Thus passion is sanctified in place and vision's very brevity – when the brother and sister turn back to look, the light is already fading – heightens desire.

Later that month, during a quiet evening as brother and sister sit reading, the unspelt peace between them is cast into relief: the firelight flickers, the watch ticks on and the keeper of the journal notes her fine obsession: 'I hear nothing else save the Breathing of my Beloved . . . ' (*AGJ*.106) A fortnight later, with William away visiting Mary, a joint letter from them pushes Dorothy close to the edge. A neighbour walks with her, questioning her like a 'catechizer', each query 'snapping a little thread about my heart'. When he leaves her alone Dorothy is able to glance up at the moon. She notes how it moves, flanked by two stars 'one larger than the other.' (*AGJ*.198) The fortunes of the two stars, never overtly linked to the two loves that bind William, wax and wane as the clouds pass over them. Through the emblematic use of the moon and stars, the landscape stands in as the anchor of personal feeling. Dorothy's emotion, rather than forging symbols set apart from the physical world, draws on the evidence of the senses to create moments of intensity that punctuate the landscape. The self and the meanings it lives by, are not readily discerniable apart from the concreteness of place.

Virgina Woolf described this absorption into the otherness of a natural landscape as a source of bliss to Dorothy, an almost mystical union that was deeply desired: 'William and Nature and Dorothy herself, were they not one being? Did they not compose a trinity, self-contained and self-sufficient and independent whether indoors or out?' (*SCR*.153) These words bring to mind the intensely feminine posture that Woolf as novelist raised to such heights. One thinks of Clarissa Dalloway stripping herself of all that can be grasped as solid and identifiable in her own nature, then touching for an instant the emptiness in the self, perfect counterpart to the moving changing reality of things. 'Women must put off their rich apparel. At mid-day they must disrobe.'[2] As with Dorothy Wordsworth, Woolf implicitly realises that the sentient self, through its abnegation of the properties of the world, is paradoxically empowered to celebrate all that lies outside its own boundaries. Yet there were darker, more disturbing forces at work for Dorothy Wordsworth, Woolf's precursor in this resolute, fragile aesthetics of sense. Absorption into otherness, even while standing as a fulfilment of what was culturally sanctioned as feminine – a modest, non-intrusive stance – drew the psyche into the grip of powerful and potentially destructive forces. Passion that could totally engulf, even as it bestowed intense value, threatened to destroy the identity-bearing structures of consciousness.

Jonathan Wordsworth has written of the private, untranslatable joy that the brother and sister sought and found in each other's company. He cites Hartley who speculated on a 'pure unmixed happiness' and the perfect instrumentality of a language capable of expressing it: 'In their personal relationship he [William] and Dorothy had achieved such a language – they were indeed "like new senses and powers of perception to each other" . . . '[3] But such bliss, bound as it was to the natural landscape could slide into terror for Dorothy when the places in which she sought an anchor for her passionate being were cut from her.

In the entry that details William's marriage to Mary in October 1802, all the wrenching insecurity of a young girl orphaned breaks loose. The journal records a near annihilation of the feeling self, an almost literal death. 'I have long loved Mary Hutchinson as a sister . . . ', Dorothy had written in a letter to Jane Pollard in September, 'but . . . I half dread that concentration of tender feelings, past, present and future, which will come upon me on the wedding morning'. She was right to be fearful. That fateful morning, paralysed by feelings that had no outlet, Dorothy lay utterly still on her bed. All the familiar moorings are cleft from her. Yet even as she recounts the silence that afflicts her sensual being, her voice is staunch, not veering from memory:

When I saw the two men running up the walk, coming to tell us it was over, I could stand it no longer and threw myself on the bed where I lay in stillness, neither hearing or seeing anything, till Sara came upstairs to me and said 'They are coming'. (*AGJ*.154)

It is as if her life were over. Her body, taking over the emotional travail that symbolic expression might have eased, lies utterly still, mimicking death. Death is a 'strange, strange, strange Scene-shifter', commented Coleridge in a letter from Germany in 1799. The loss of his infant son Berkeley was vivid in his mind as he set out the dizzying insecurity of death that 'so unsubstantiates the living Things that one has grasped and handled!' He turns then to 'A Slumber did my Spirit seal', which Wordsworth had sent him, speculating that the poem 'a most sublime Epitaph' was probably based in the poet's deep dejection as Wordsworth 'fancied the moment in which his Sister might die.' (*CL*.1:479)

In this conjunction of all engulfing passion and death, Coleridge may well have touched on a raw nerve in Wordsworth's intimate bond. But it is clear that her brother's marriage, in spite of all the tenderness Dorothy felt for Mary Hutchinson, must have been intensely threatening. The scenes of her life had radically shifted, and her feeling self was cut loose from a known existence. Seeking in her brother a reparation for early loss of a home, she had made the choice to turn towards him and the privacy of their love, rejecting a world outside that might have offered her a personal vindication.

*   *   *

In the early journals the present tense is most frequently employed in sharp, fragmented observations. But Dorothy turns to the past in one long narrative entry to record a fateful journey she undertook with her brother. Almost three months earlier on July 9, 1802 they had set off from Grasmere and in a long outward trajectory, made their way to France. The meeting with Annette Vallon, William's French lover and the sight of Caroline, her brother's illegitimate daughter, must have touched Dorothy deeply. In letters of 1793 that make painful reading, Annette writes to the lover who had left her with a young child to return to his homeland; she evokes a woman she has never met. She must respond to Dorothy's letter, writes Annette: 'La terre n'en a pas produit deux comme elle; elle fait l'honneur de son sexe. Je désire bien que ma Caroline lui resemble. Que j'ai pleuré, mon cher Williams!'[4] Dorothy had earlier counselled and supported the unseen Annette, but in the 1802 journal entry she turns quiet. Mistress of indirection, she merely makes a factual note of meeting the mother and child, of walking with them by the shore. Her emotion is focused on the purple brilliance of waves by the Calais coast, 'brighter than precious stones for ever melting away . . . '; the evening stars; the wooden fort at the harbour mouth. Back in England, 'many a melancholy and tender thought' is as much as she can acknowledge of her journey. (*AGJ*.152,153)

From Dover, the brother and sister travelled to Gallow Hill for the simple marriage ceremony, then with Mary Hutchinson turned back to Grasmere. The difficult journey homewards required the distancing memory can offer. Through its sensuous continuity Dorothy regained a hold on her self, hardly as stable as that which the outer landscape might provide, but crucial nevertheless as a support. Through memory the world outside was recast in terms of what has already been, a process which can sometimes distance and heal, reconciling the bewildered consciousness to its own fate. Its use then, in this long narrative passage of the *Grasmere Journal*, while shorn of the mythopoeic activity that characterises William Wordsworth's use of the faculty, serves Dorothy well. It permits her to order emotions that might otherwise have laid her self utterly waste.

The trip back to Grasmere is hard. The three travellers are flung against each other in a jolting carriage, the women succumbing to sickness caused by the abrupt motion. Acutely conscious that she is returning to a beloved home that has changed, Dorothy searches for a stay. She sees again, if only briefly, places previously visited. These small recognitions summon up a poignant joy – the inn outside Helmsley with its bright yellow walls; a valley by the Hambledon Hills, site of her brother's sonnets; Wensley, a stopping place that doubles back for her in memory as an intense 'inner vision'. She writes that her heart 'melted away' at the sight of the village with its bridge, waterspout, hill and church, their value bound into what they had prefigured when almost three years ago she

stood in the very same spot with William, looking forward
to life in Grasmere, the 'home in which we were to rest.'
(*AGJ*.158)

Shortly afterwards, as her reflections gather momentum,
she evokes the earth itself as a home, a natural harbour
akin to the maternal body that first succoured life. This
habitable landscape has 'little openings upon recesses and
concealed retreats'. Elsewhere she speaks of Grasmere with
bowers and parlours 'not *enclosed* by walls' and resting
places shaped out of the very stuff of earth, 'soft green
cradles, hollows surrounded with green grassy hillocks'.
(*AGJ*.158,115,155) Within these natural enclosures she
finds emblems of her own being, the private fragmented
self of the writing woman metamorphosed, if only for an
instant, into the precious sight of blossoms that cling to
their own survival.

Coming upon a strawberry blossom Dorothy unthink-
ingly uproots it, then feeling she has committed an 'outrage'
replants it in the earth, its rightful shelter. 'It will have a
stormy life of it' she muses 'but let it live if it can.' (*AGJ*.83)
The act of rooting the plant after having torn it out must
have touched her deeply. It moves her to greater humility
when she sees the columbine, its emblematic status overtly
drawn: 'a solitary plant . . . a graceful slender creature, a
female seeking retirement and growing freest and most
graceful where it is most alone.' (*AGJ*.129) A protected
solitude, 'sheltered and shaded by the tufts and Bowers
of trees' permits the plant to flourish. The woman writer's
Romanticism discovers in the organic development of a wild
flower a fit emblem of her potentialities, flourishing when
most private, most free of the constraints of society with
its 'Ridicule or Censure'.

Now that the earlier fantasy of the shared cottage with her
brother has touched ground, its actuality mingling with the
complexities of their shared lives, Dorothy moves outward,
away from a cottage fitted out with stones and mortar, into

silent, secluded spots in the landscape, seeking images of a natural benevolence that permits vulnerable forms of life to survive. The columbine exists within the natural landscape without being absorbed into it, emblem of a poise where selfhood is not consumed by a circumambient otherness that should support it. Close to the end of her *Grasmere Journals* she notes a tuft of primroses. There are 'three flowers in full blossom and a Bud'. (*AGJ*.164) She is glad of the decision not to pluck them, to let them 'live out their day', for returning, she sees them still 'uninjured', persisting in their natural shelter.

It is within such a shelter untouched by cultural constraints, rather than in the cottage of her earlier fantasies, that Dorothy Wordsworth marks her most acute perceptions of coming home. Her passionate being turns away from a world that would deny it, entering instead into a green world that endures for imaginative knowledge. In the entry for April 29, 1802 she tells of how brother and sister walked out to John's Grove. They find a 'trench', a shallow depression under the fence capable of holding the bodies of both siblings. So they lie there utterly still, just hearing each other breathe, entering into an almost prelapsarian bliss, as if the womb of a lost mother held them both. Dorothy finely attuned as always to her brother's feelings describes him: 'with his eyes shut and listening to the waterfalls and the Birds . . . William heard me breathing and rustling now and then but we both lay still, and unseen, by one another.' (*AGJ*.117) A hospitable furrow in the earth's body harbours a love that the cottage could not sustain.

They lie there, their twinned bodies not touching, the unseen waterfalls blending in sound, till what is heard is 'the voice of the air'. Wordsworth is moved to thoughts of the grave; not a pit of dissolution, but the heart of a peaceful kingdom: 'It would be as sweet thus to lie so in the grave to hear the *peaceful* sounds of the earth and just to know that our dear friends were near.' Later that

day, in seemingly unconscious repetition the brother and
sister lie down again, this time under a wall, and now
it is Dorothy who is pushed to the brink of her being,
glimpsing a curious metamorphosis. Through the action
of sunlight, sheep those everyday creatures of Grasmere,
are subtly changed into 'animals of another kind – as if
belonging to a more splendid world.' (*AGJ*.117)

'Floating Island': Sinking and Surviving

Linguistic images that tell of dwelling and shelter as crucial
to our tenure on earth abound in Dorothy Wordsworth's
writings. In her subtle, inimitable way she refined her
concerns to the primary ones of shelter and dwelling,
themes intrinsic to her survival as an expressive being.
From the psychological and sexual marginality forced on
her as a single woman in the early Romantic era, she forged
natural emblems, depicted topographies that are pitted with
instability, in turn sheltering and displacing consciousness.
The maternal powers of nature could never be taken for
granted. But the compulsion to be absorbed into otherness
that Woolf recognised – whether into the landscape or into
her passion for William – stands in tension with an opposing
posture, the longing to keep separate and distinct. In the
fragile, natural objects she celebrated in her journals,
Dorothy wished her woman's self kept intact, free from
external compulsions, living and moving without torsion
or taint. Hence the image of the columbine in the *Grasmere
Journals* and the emblematic power of the plant as female,
thriving in a sheltered solitude.

Yet survival in a sheltered place, rooted well if in
marked fragility, is only one moment within the complex
span of her work. Such rootedness has to contend with a
natural flux that permeated the world for her, a continual
inconstancy that she spelt out in her moving images of light

and wind and water. At times this flux condemned her to a knife-edge existence between changefulness that could grant a freedom from entrapment and a displacement so radical that it could uproot and destroy, fulfilling those terrors of early orphancy that still clung to her under the surfaces of everyday life.

Dorothy Wordsworth's poem 'Floating Island' was published in her own lifetime but anonymously within the corpus of her brother's work. (*PW*.4:162-3) The poem enacts a symbolic destruction of substance. The island, a tiny 'slip of earth' is cut loose by wind and water from the mothering hold of a mossy shore. 'Dissevered' it is entirely obedient to the wind that had first 'undermined' it and brought it to an autonomous existence. The fierce emotion glimpsed in this second stanza is at variance with the poem's opening where curiously neutral tones are employed. The voice tells of 'Sunshine and cloud, whirlwind and breeze' that work in harmony with nature. Indeed nature's power both to bring into existence and to annihilate is underlined in a subtitle preserved in the manuscript, but omitted from the published version. 'Floating Island at Hawkshead, An Incident in the schemes of Nature' we read in Dorothy's careful hand.[5] Her choice of the word 'schemes' seems deliberate, implying perhaps a destructive will beneath the randomness of natural power.

The island, a tiny fragment of land, complete with a 'crest of trees' provides nourishment to a blooming, buzzing life: 'There berries ripen, flowerets bloom;/There insects live their lives, and die'. Yet a vitality that holds and preserves disparate forms of life is no guarantee against extinction. Though a 'peopled world', the island is minute no larger than a 'tiny room'. One day it is swallowed up in water. The arbitrary power of nature, functions ceaselessly, independently of human awareness. This natural power which is clearly marked as female condemns the island to groundlessness. The poet's 'I', invoked when the island came into being, dissolves into the generalised 'we' as the voice attempts to account for the cruel destruction of substance. In the penultimate stanza the reader is evoked, one who must stand as witness to this death. With a mind perfectly cleansed of all attachment and emotion such a witness can mark the island's vanishing. Defined as ontological lack, the island emerges for consciousness through the very fact of having vanished, a negativity to existence. To exist is to appear to consciousness, and the island incapable of appearing, no longer exists.

'It is the property of fortitude not to be easily terrified by the dread of things pertaining to death . . . ', Dorothy had written in her Commonplace Book, an axiom surely taken to heart here.[6] A stoical courage underwrites her voice, telling of itself through an island condemned to annihilation, since it has nowhere to be. To exist, one must be in place, and the island has vanished: 'Its place no longer to be found'. The tentative emotion at the poem's end is vested in the continuance of 'lost fragments' that might persist, and perhaps someday 'fertilise some other ground'.

The poem haunted its author. The vanished ground imaged in it, drawing on her marginality as a writing woman, came to evoke her own pitiful condition in those last two and a half decades of her life when she was crippled by illness, confined to her bedchamber at Allan Bank or wheeled about its gardens. In a note to the poem William Wordsworth observed the pleasure she took in repeating 'those verses' which 'My poor sister . . . composed not long before the beginning of her illness.' (PW.4,438)

During those terrible years, her mind wandering, her thoughts at times deranged, Dorothy often repeated fragments of the poetry she had composed or recited others she had learnt. Her brother makes no connection between the floating island she evokes and his own use of the image in The Prelude. The connection however is instructive. 'A floating island, an amphibious thing/Unsound of spongy texture . . . ', wrote the poet, evoking a time when his creativity was in limbo, his contemplative memory almost stopped up. (*Prel*.III:340-1) In his *Guide to the Lakes*, Wordsworth alludes to a floating or 'Buoyant Island' – a curious mass of gases and waterweeds – that can spring up suddenly under the water's surface.[7] In *The Prelude* this phenomenon, visible often on Derwent Water for instance, takes on an ambivalent value. Neither solid earth nor water, the island lacks a place in the hierarchies of existence. Its 'amphibious' nature frustrates the territorial impulses of a poet who must achieve a firm imaginative hold over the surrounding landscape in order to compose. To liken his own self during his Cambridge days to such an island, is to discover in its floating existence an image of poetic frustration, a fatal lack of coordinates, a loss of that 'appropriate human centre' which seemed essential. (*Prel*.IV:359) Yet what was 'unsound' to her brother, was the condition of life as lived to Dorothy and in making the island the emotive centre of her poem, she perfectly evokes a marginal existence, its inner resources helpless when faced with powers that can displace and destroy. If there is hope in her poem, it lies under water, in the lost fragments preserved there.

Dorothy was well aware that water was symbolic of maternity. In the Commonplace Book, in pages copied in from Barrow's *Travels in China*, we see references to a waterborne deity, the '*Shing-Moo*' or '*Mother of perfect intelligence*', who in one of her forms resides on the leaves of the *Nelumbrium*, a blossoming, water-borne plant like the lotus. Having eaten of its blossom the deity gave birth to a son, who in mythic fashion grew up and performed great deeds. The civilisations of Egypt, India and China are said to have paid homage to avatars of this goddess, who combined the qualities of maternal nurturance with great intelligence. In Dorothy's careful hand one reads that

water, the medium on which the '*Shing-Moo*' is borne, is
considered 'to be the primary element, and the first medium
on which the creative influence began to act'.[8]

*   *   *

Of the floating island, only shards survive. In a series
of poems in her later Commonplace Book ('A Sketch', 'A
Cottage in Grasmere Vale', 'After Recollection at sight of the
same Cottage') Dorothy charts a more substantial survival.[9]
The central image of the cottage opens up tensions that recur
in her writings: between security and its loss, between being
embedded as if in maternal soil and the painful displacement
wrought by natural processes.

A house, writes Gaston Bachelard, 'constitutes a body of
images that give mankind proofs or illusions of stability.'[10]
In Dorothy's cottage poems, the stability of the dwelling
place is cut by emblems of motion, either a road the 'serpent
line' of 'A Sketch' – or the wind and storm. But the cottage,
well encircled by natural topography, is never engulfed. In
'A Sketch', it becomes a 'little nest', well girded by a 'tuft
of flourishing trees'. The road that draws forward, image of
solitary quest, leads to the cottage but rises beyond it. With
stasis and motion held in tension, the poet's consciousness
can maintain a necessary poise, neither imprisoned nor
radically displaced. As visible symbols of the bodily self,
Dorothy's cottages are modest, unobtrusive, partially veiled
from the world's glare. Unlike her brother's enigmatic Lucy
('a violet in a mossy grove/half-hidden from the eye'), they
are almost but not quite, absorbed into the natural setting.
They linger in the landscape as counterparts to the 'parlour
not made with hands', the nooks and crannies in the
landscape that Dorothy once discovered as brief shelters
for fragile forms of life.

In 'A Cottage in Grasmere Vale' a 'lowly shed' that
seems to be 'the very mountain's child' entices the speaker.

Its wildness is fit counterpart to the speaker's 'fancy', which is characterised as 'unfettered – wild – '. The fields that encircle the dwelling, presumably portions of the human world of order, are scarcely fields; they are 'craggy, steep and bare'. In the third stanza we read: 'Their fence is of the mountain stone/And moss and lichen flourish there.' The raw stuff of a maternal nature protects the dwelling from the ferocity of storm and wind. The active, moving processes of nature threaten but cannot destroy the cottage. It persists, much like the female body, encircled by the already given materials of the world. The tension Coleridge envisaged between the *natura naturata*, the solid, already formed stuff of nature and the *natura naturans*, or active moving spirit of nature, seems acutely relevant to Dorothy's poetic vision. Yet there is an obvious difference.

While Coleridge in his essay 'On Poesy or Art' counsels the artist to 'master the essence, the *natura naturans*', Dorothy Wordsworth, his friend and contemporary envisages a less hierarchial, more supple bond between poetic consciousness and its subject matter.[11] The symbolic violence implicit in the Coleridgean imagination finds no place in Dorothy's work. Her non-confrontational stance preserves at its heart an interplay between the solid, already given landscape and the moving quick of her chosen elements, wind or water. Lacking this interplay, which at times slips from liveliness to an irresolute back and forth, the pregiven world imprisons and objectifies the woman's consciousness. In the cottage poems, the wind is essential. It quickens the earth's solidities. Without it, the cottage would quickly turn from a shelter into a prison. The brief concluding poem of the series, 'After Recollection at sight of the same cottage', stands as a coda to the previous poem. The storm has passed, the wind assumes a 'gentle sway', and the speaker is able to hear 'a solitary throstle sing'.

In the Commonplace Book, a longer poem follows

directly: 'A Winter's Ramble in Grasmere Vale'.[12] The
thematics of spatial form glimpsed earlier return but with
a telling variation. Instead of a cottage – a space that can
be entered into and might well shelter the female body –
the poetic speaker confronts the opaque surfaces of a great
rock whose massive solidity permits no escape. Lured by a
'little winding path' the speaker has climbed eastward, up
a height. She finds herself face to face with a 'stately rock'
covered with moss and ferns, garlanded with eglantine,
foxglove, and 'hips of glossy red'. The monumental rock
effectively stops the wanderer. She is forced to gaze up
at its summit and recognise its 'splendid garb'. If there is
something almost grotesque in this huge apparition, it is
unacknowledged in the words the speaker addresses to it.
A 'stranger' in Grasmere, she is thrust back into her grief
at the passing of summer, an allusion one imagines to her
own past and the loss of its 'pleasure gardens'. An almost
fatal lack of energy seems to invade her, and the voice
resorts to rhetoric: 'What need of flowers?' Having lost
the possibility of motion the speaker turns back on her
own emotions and rejects their painful complexity. The
stream by her, commands her to rejoice.

In *The Romantic Mother*, Barbara Schapiro argues that
Wordsworth in his poetry is powerfully impelled not so
much to recapture the lost mother as 'to fortify the self
in relation to her, to become a power like her . . . '[13]
At times, his creative power seeks to displace or usurp
nature's. With Dorothy however, the natural powers that
encircle the feminine self, can never be seized. Almost as
if they were part of the woman's very flesh, they strike out
a painful self-division in the speaker. Faced with the rock
into which she can never enter, the speaker discovers herself
stuck, all volition lost. She must make the best of it. She
muses on her earlier longings now 'matured by thoughtful
choice'. Pleasure, scarcely self-evident, must be willed as
best she can:

> I stood an *Inmate* of this Vale,
> How *could* I but rejoice?

The irony is not lost on the poet. Her deliberate emphasis on '*Inmate*' hints at the imprisoning nature of a valley which leaves her with nowhere to go. The real, solid world as she faces it, is sullied by a loss of freedom, a paralysing lack of mobility. The heavy furniture of the actual distresses her. It could even be argued that the deliberate act of walking up the hill towards the rock is cause for imaginative grief. She is 'lured': clearly a narrative device employed to cast the real goal of her quest into relief. Loss of serendipity entails loss of power. The woman writer's capabilities here are most acute when least dependent on the already given structure of things. What is discovered as one goes along, quite by accident, is most capable of instilling order.

These poems play out a tension within the poet's feminine self, rather than confronting, as Margaret Homans has suggested of the cottage poems, a source of power external to her own, 'the centralising imagination that her brother possesses and that she lacks and hardly dare to appropriate.' Homans sees in the cottage a place the speaker is barred from, a figure for the 'subjectivity that she requires in order to have the poetic imagination'. Dorothy's own consciousness in this critical reading has merely 'the devalued fancy that flits from one vantage point to the next'.[14] Yet in these poems, it seems to me, Dorothy is forging a trope for her own precarious poise rather than struggling with her brother's egocentric power for which she exists as a secondary being. The interplay between stability and flux displays the tensions she faced as a writing woman, one who struggled with an acute sense of not having a place in the world. Yet there are moments of joy in her work, when an altogether unworldly sense of being at home in the world is granted her. This Romantic capacity for renewal in nature tugs Dorothy away from a quarrel with the world and its public forms of power, away too from the realm that a feminist consciousness requires. Finally her consciousness seems orphaned, enclosed in its privacy.

George and Sarah Green: A Loss of Ground

Lucy Snowe, protagonist of Charlotte Brontë's *Villette*, published in 1853 two years before Dorothy's death, muses on her feminine condition, her 'homeless, anchorless, unsupported mind'.[15] Driven by her anguished self-consciousness, Lucy passes through the manifold humiliations thrust on her as a woman who must make her own way in the world, quite unprotected. Yet at the end, in a curious, strengthening ambivalence, she holds together the conflicting realms of love and work the fruit of an acute, self-scrutinising consciousness and that capable, resolute existence which is also hers as a woman struggling to maintain her work in the public world. For Dorothy Wordsworth however, born almost a half century before Brontë, love and work blended into each other. Both flourished in the half-darkness of a deliberately chosen privacy, lacking which the writing woman could not have conceived of her own existence. Or so it seems as one considers her letter of December 1810 to Catherine Clarkson, clearly setting out the reasons why she did not want to publish her narrative *George and Sarah Green*: 'I should detest the idea of setting myself up as an Author.'

It is not only that Dorothy's personal existence would be damaged by taking on a public and professional status, but also that the lives of the orphaned children, the subjects of her narrative, might be irretrievably damaged. The event seems to her 'too recent to be published in delicacy to others'. After the passage of thirty or forty years, she adds, the narrative might well be published; no one could possibly be

Blake frontispiece for Wollstonecraft's *Original Stories*.
Photograph © Henry W. and Albert A. Berg Collection,
The New York Public Library, Astor, Lenox and Tilden
Foundations

Opie portrait of Mary Wollstonecraft.
Photograph © The National Portrait Gallery

Silhouette of Dorothy Wordsworth.
Photograph © Dove Cottage Trust, Grasmere

Amos Green drawing of Dove Cottage.
Photograph © Dove Cottage Trust, Grasmere

Proof portrait of Mary Shelley (Ashley MS 5022, X).
Photograph © The British Library

Shelley house in San Terenzo (Ashley MS 5022, XIX)
Photograph © The British Library

harmed then. (*MY*.454) Her thoughts characteristically are for others, for other lives bound with hers in a relational existence. Yet such a life, for all its ethical viability, can breed pain and confusion in matters where an autonomous sense of self is required.

Certainly for Dorothy Wordsworth the feminine, nurturing virtues were in conflict with the public estate of authorship. As a woman she grasped the public world as inimical to her expressive self and thought it best not to enter it. A further reason underlies the refusal to publish. This too, she asserts, is 'entirely disconnected with myself'. She explains that if her narrative had been an 'invention of my own it might have been published without a name, and nobody would have thought of me'. Since, however, it deals with the actual lives of the Greens, she cannot consent to publication. (*MY*.454)

While consonant with her fear of hurting the orphans through unwanted publicity, her reasoning points to a darker, more distrustful theme. Had she merely invented the story, she would feel able to publish it, to grant it a public existence though one in which her own part remained anonymous. But as it represents actuality, things as they are, she does not feel capable of publishing it. Her enforced marginality exacts a terrible price.

One must bear in mind that for William Wordsworth, who defined a poetic centrality for himself, events that actually occurred became the very stuff of art. In *The Prelude* he implicitly contrasts this imaginatively fulfilling existence with what he thought of as the painful insubstantiality of Coleridge's life. Coleridge, exiled from nature as a child was condemned to a reflexivity without outlet, a 'self-created sustenance'. Mere words for him took the place of a substantial life. All he could create was a patchwork of 'things well-matched or ill'. (*Prel*.VI:311,312)

While Dorothy was not exiled from the natural landscape, in the way her brother considered Coleridge to be, the anguish that underlies her authorial anonymity has similar roots, at least in relation to her brother's genius. The creative others closest to Wordsworth often suffered an involuntary diminishment. But gender is crucial. As a woman Dorothy chose a public silence, quite far from Coleridge's continual self-dramatisation. But the very privacy that enabled her to clarify the workings of her feminine consciousness, worked against that part of her expressive self that might seek an acknowledged life as a writer.

To Thomas De Quincey who admired her deeply, Dorothy Wordsworth was a woman divided against herself. He notes how her feminine powers were incorporated into her brother's genius, how she willingly ministers to him to 'ingraft by her sexual sense of beauty, upon his masculine austerity' her unique delicacy and grace. (R.201) And here De Quincey has recourse to the passage in *The Prelude* (the poem still in manuscript as he points out) where Wordsworth compares his own genius to a crag, fierce and awe-inspiring, but softened by the gentle domestic arts that his sister had perfected.

To De Quincey, his relations with the Wordsworths already strained, it was clear that Dorothy's writing self was permanently compromised by this absorption of her talents into her brother's poetic estate. He reflects on her name, its meaning in Greek 'gift of God' which seems to him to 'prefigure the relation in which she stood to Wordsworth, the mission with which she was charged – to wait upon him as the tenderest and most faithful of domestics . . . ' (R.201) Later in the same chapter of his *Recollections*, in an effort to account for the sad course of her life, De Quincey, sensitised no doubt by his own considerable anguish, observes that Dorothy might have done much better as a 'bluestocking' or 'a writer for the press'; that it might have eased her pain to have chosen a more public existence. He mentions Joanna Baillie and Miss

Mitford, two contemporary women writers who pursued the 'profession of authorship' with 'absolutely no sacrifice or loss of feminine dignity'. (*R*.205) Such a life, devoted to a professional and hence more autonomous existence, might have supported Dorothy's mind, kept it from that 'nervous depression which, I grieve to hear, has clouded her later days.' (*R*.205)

By the time De Quincey published his essay, Dorothy had sunk into her crippling 'Wilderness' of thought. We read the poignant complaint addressed to her 'dearest Dora'. She must write a letter, and what can she put in it but 'News – news I must seek for news. My own thoughts are a wilderness.' Her friends Peggy Benson, Fanny Haigh and Mrs Rawson are dead. She survives, worn down to the bone: '*I* have fought and fretted and striven – and am here beside the fire.' She writes of the doves behind her at the window, the laburnum pods shivering, the pine trees that 'rock from their base'. (*LY*.528)

★   ★   ★

Dorothy Wordsworth as a young woman turned to what seemed most precious to her, both reparation and fulfilment within William's 'coverture'. The term, used by Sir William Blackstone to describe the legal cover afforded the wife by her husband, so complete that it could absorb her separate identity, seems appropriate when considering Dorothy's life as a writing woman. Her brother's influence is visible in the headnote he composed for her precise, poignant narrative of 1808, *George and Sarah Green*. He explains that the work was composed by Dorothy at the 'request of her brother' and sets out the manner in which the document is to be read: as a 'record of human sympathies and moral sentiments'.[16] His words point towards a moral idealism consonant with his thought at the time. In a letter of April 18, 1808, less than a month before the headnote was composed, Wordsworth wrote to Coleridge about the tragic death of the Greens. He includes a ballad composed for the occasion, then reflects on his own long poem *The White Doe of Rylstone*, which preoccupied him greatly at the time. He tells of Emily whose suffering alone raises her up, out of the tormenting earthly realm, rendering her a woman to be 'honoured and loved for what she *endures*, and the manner in which she endures it . . . ' (*MY*.222)

It is in the same vein that he penned his prefatory note to his sister's narrative. But Wordsworth's concern with 'moral sentiments' stands at odds with the lucid, moving account she renders of death and human suffering, where pain is endured but without any overt reaching after spirituality. Dorothy's account of the tragic deaths of George and Sarah Green focuses in large part on maternal loss. It was a topic that made sense to her in more ways than one. Quite apart from her own early orphancy, the woman writer discovered in the concrete, day to day concerns of maternity a locus of uniquely female power. Furthermore, it was a power that lay within the keeping of woman's sphere of activity. Her refusal to publish her narrative was really a refusal to enter the realm of authorship where the public and patriarchal worlds intersected. But in the maternal powers she discovered a space that her feminine, nonconfrontational sensibility could draw strength from. And it was here at the heart of the domestic and private that she found an arena of action. Maternity is imaged in her work most intensely in its absence, as radical loss. The annihilation of the floating island has its counterpart in the abyss that draws the Greens to their death.

The death of a mother was something she knew from the inside. Though she never had children of her own, mothering became for her a way of reparation, a way of fulfilling her considerable powers of care-giving. Instructing the young was part of her quasi-maternal functions. As a teenager, living with her uncle William Cookson, she participated in the instruction of girls at Sunday School. There were plans that never came to fruition for a larger more ambitious institution, 'a sort of School of Industry' that Dorothy would run with her aunt. (*EY*.67) Later, living with William and Mary she embraced their growing family as her own. Acutely sensitive to the needs of the young, she found in childhood a fit emblem of human joy and its brevity. 'Still bound together in one knot/Beneath your tender Mother's eye', she wrote in a late poem on the nostalgic pleasures of childhood.[17] But though at times the maternal power to harbour and preserve coincided with the sheltering capacities of nature that 'careful Warder', often as not death cut in.[18]

Maternity is identified with places that permit of being, with the earth itself as harbour. The loss of the maternal hold becomes loss of ground. In *George and Sarah Green*, the death of the mother is repeated in an abyssal figuration the voice cannot control. Inevitably the survival of the orphaned children is called into question. But the very problem of their survival is what requires Dorothy's narrative to come into being, her overt purpose being to gather money for them. In a detailed preface, borne out by the notes preserved in the Wordsworth Library, de Selincourt, the editor of *George and Sarah Green*, sets out the careful attempts to raise money for the children and the conflicting emotions aroused by the efforts of disparate members of the Committee of Ladies who were to supervise the collection of money and placement of the children. Dorothy Wordsworth was one of the most active of this small group of women. At the practical level her narrative was a document designed to elicit further support for the orphans. As such it gave her an imaginative permission she might otherwise have lacked to draw deep on the pain of a mother's death.

In *George and Sarah Green*, the authorial focus is on the mother, Sarah Green, and beyond her on a mode of

care giving, characteristically maternal. The infant clings
to Jane, the oldest daughter left in the house. Jane's
labour is crucial to the survival of the orphaned children.
The poignancy of her fate is insisted on: Jane who had to
become 'Mother to her Brothers and Sisters when they were
fatherless and motherless'. (*GSG*.66) She feeds the younger
children, milks the cow, makes sure that the fire still burns
in the house, all with a 'calmness amounting to dignity'.
(*GSG*.67) The turbulence of the child's own feelings never
show through. The narrator does not even hint at them.
Rather her beauty and grace are depicted. But the house
itself is '*afflicted*'. (*GSG*.52) An earlier mother, George
Green's first wife had died there of an infectious fever.
Her son grown now, always referred to Sarah Green as
'*Mother*'. (*GSG*.86) Shocked by the sudden loss of his
father and step-mother he fainted at the very threshold
of his own house, and might have perished in the cold,
the narrator tells us, had his voice not been heard by his
wife. Continuing a train of thought, the narrator quotes
from Wordworth's poem: 'I may say with the Pedlar in
the "Recluse" ':

> "I feel
> The story linger in my heart, my memory
> clings to this poor Woman and her family."
> (*GSG*.86)

'*Excursion*, 1.777-80 (misquoted)', de Selincourt tells us
in a footnote. But the misquotation is telling. 'My spirit
clings/To that poor woman . . . ' the narrator said of
Margaret, a woman who seemed to him 'By sorrow laid
asleep; or borne away . . . ' (*PW*.5:34) By adding 'her
family' Dorothy highlights a maternal strength that survives
even through tragedy. William Wordsworth's emphasis on
the sublimity to be gained by bearing witness to Margaret's
sufferings – the soul gaining subtly from another's earthly

pain – is turned around in Dorothy's memory. Her emphasis is on the here and now, the terrible, inviolably concrete deprivation suffered by the children in Sarah Green's family. The author must nurture them as best she can through the power of the written word.

A Narrative Concerning George and Sarah Green of the Parish of Grasmere, Addressed to a Friend, opens in remarkably direct fashion invoking a 'You' familiar with the landscape around Easedale and the Green cottage at Blentarn Gill that stands to this day with a little stream rushing past the garden wall. The narrator even suggests that the couple who died so tragically might have been known to the reader. George and Sarah Green had travelled away from home to attend a sale in Langdale, a social event that was of great importance to Sarah: for the 'main object for the *woman's* journey at least . . . was to see her Daughter who was in service there . . . ' (*GSG*.43-4) This young woman was Sarah's 'natural' daughter, born out of wedlock and nurtured by her without patriarchal protection. It was only later that Sarah married the widowed George Green.

The narrator herself enters into the text when she observes the landscape where the couple lost their lives. The spot in the mountains where the man and woman had left their footprints – now covered over with fresh snow – at the top of Blea Crag, was clearly visible: 'that very spot where I myself had sate down six years ago, unable to see a yard before me . . . ' Parting from her brother at Stickle Tarn the narrator had wandered in the mist quite lost. When the mist cleared she found herself 'at the edge of the Precipice and trembled at the Gulph below which appeared immeasurable.' (*GSG*.45,46) It was still day, and she was able in her long walk home to restore herself. But the reader cannot easily forget the 'Gulph' in the earth into which the narrator had almost slipped. A minute graphic detail – one of the 'sad hieroglyphics' De Quincey refers to in his 'Recollections of Grasmere' – follows on: we are told of the dead man's fractured skull, then a single shoe belonging to Sarah Green, left behind above the precipice, a mute reminder of mortality. (*R*.264)

Sarah 'had rolled many yards down the breast of the hill. Her body was terribly bruised.' The narrator's own fears ('recollecting my own dreadful situation') are uncannily confirmed. The loss of ground results in a woman's death. She had rolled down the 'breast' of land. It did not prevent her fall. A few lines later we read that it was 'well known' in the community that 'if the Mother had been *alive* she would have returned to her sucking Babe . . . ' (*GSG*.47-8) In each case a maternal power cuts itself away, severely damaging the possibilities of survival for a dependant other. The hill's breast allows the woman, surely nature's child, to roll to her death. The woman in turn, severs her breast from the helpless 'sucking Babe' whose lips might go on sucking, but over mere air, closed on nothingness.

The death of a mother was taken in so deeply by the narrator that to tell of it at all was to repeat it, helplessly almost, in frame after frame of the narrative. So the tale, to reach a suitable closure travels through Sarah's death, the mortal affliction of the Green house, the premature transformation of a girl child into a mother-surrogate, and then through a series of endnotes that the writer appended to her narrative, textual doublings to her brother's head-note. In that note he authorised her to write in '*minute detail*' all that she had observed. In her endnotes she counters with concrete but disconnected facts that strike her: the meaning of Blentarn Gill ('Blind Tarn', she surmises); the four pounds of butter Sarah had once brought up for Dorothy; the utter lack of provisions in the Green household – we recall the family's dire poverty, forced to cut into the land, 'their own heart's heart', for a few peats to sell for ready money. (*GSG*.49) From the economy of survival, the writer turns to Sarah's 'natural daughter', the young woman evoked at the start of the narrative. It was to see her that the mother had specially travelled to the sale. The daughter, we are told had to be kept 'with difficulty' from racing up the snow covered mountains to search for her lost mother.

Through the indirections of narrative technique the second endnote moves from house/body emptied out by poverty and death and the sale of a few household objects, to a daughter's grief at maternal loss. As if in associated thought ('I believe most young persons in the like dreadful situation would have felt in the same manner – and perhaps old ones too . . . '), the narrative goes on to a tragedy that struck Mary Watson, an old woman, aged seventy-three when her son died. Unable to swim, the young man had drowned in 'one of the well-springs of the lake which are always very deep'. The narrator recalls 'standing close to her': the harrowed mother wringing her hands in grief, too numb even to weep.

Then follows a pencilled note, scribbled, as one sees in the manuscript in a jagged, distraught fashion, quite in contrast to the firm, clear, inked in words one reads in the body of her text.[19] It was obviously pencilled in by Dorothy as de Selincourt suggests at 'a much later date'. The note, which effectively concludes the text as we have it in manuscript form, tells of Mary Watson and the violent death she suffered at the hand of her crazed son, a 'poor Maniac' with whom she shared her home. After a daughter's pain at her mother's death, the voice moves to a mother's grief at her lost child, fulfilling a tragic symmetry. Yet this structural closure is abruptly destroyed by the scribbled endnote which tells the gruesome facts of matricide. While it is quite possible that Dorothy jotted in 'the end of Mary Watson . . . more tragical than that of the young man' as it actually occurred, adding it sequentially to her narrative, one wonders if this might have been the only way in which she could close her narrative: uncontainable loss at a mother's death, turned round in sheer anger; a child's outrage at abandonment turned to a figural abyss that finally destroys '*Mother*', first shelter and most perfect place of incorporation.

6 Unnatural Creation

A Monstrous Double (*Frankenstein*)

Just a year after Shelley's 'Alastor' (1816), the young Mary Godwin subjected her lover's vision of limitless spiritual ascendancy, of a double born out of sheer desire, to a fierce and implacable scrutiny. Obsessed by the quest for 'immortality and power', Victor Frankenstein turns to the charnel house, fitting together bits and pieces of dead bodies, struggling to create new life. Through his assiduous labour he uncovers the 'cause of generation', then moves forward to forge a new species of man (*F*.46,52) Yet this double of flesh and blood imbues him with disgust, its grotesque, ill-proportioned body mocking his endeavour. Instead of feeling compassion for the being he has created, he flees it in terror.

Ellen Moers reflects on how the novel *Frankenstein* (1818) is 'distinctly a *woman's* mythmaking on the subject of birth precisely because its emphasis is . . . upon what follows birth: the trauma of the afterbirth.'[1] A dark double, its materiality never to be drawn back into the recesses of consciousness, the monster haunts its creator. Where Percy Shelley had envisioned a sexual counterpart, a feminine, febrile spirit who has nothing to do with the realms of physicality, Mary Shelley, her young body already scarred by the birth of her firstborn (a girl, born on February 22, 1815, survived only till March 6) forges a double of skin and blood and guts, mottled and misshapen. The monster, as the world calls him, for he never received a name, becomes a 'fatal secret' that dominates Victor's life (*F*.185)

Towards the end of the novel Elizabeth Lavenza, Victor's adopted sister, pure, virtuous, long-suffering, filled with love for the man she is to marry, finally asks him: 'Do you not love another?' Her question is well placed. It requires the 'utmost self-violence' in Victor to keep the monster secret. Yet such secrecy by concealing the murderous rage of the monster, protects Frankenstein's own implacable ambition, turned bitter now, but still fiercely excluding the healing that might come from a shared love. (*F*.187,186) Victor has abandoned the monster in his helpless infancy – if one may use such a term here for the full grown, hefty size of the creation – and then aborted the female counterpart that the monster longs for. In all this 'filthy process' the laboratory has taken the place of the womb. The circumvention of normal sexuality and procreation, a process in which female physicality is intrinsically involved, results in a hideous maternity conducted with scalpel and suturing devices. Robert Kiely convincingly argues that while Mary Shelley has little problem in according Victor god-like attributes, his real presumption in the novel, lies 'in his attempt to usurp the power of women.'[2]

The monster, who has sworn revenge, murders Elizabeth on her wedding night. (*F*.164) Victor discovers her dishevelled corpse draped over the bed. A train of destruction follows. At the novel's end Walton, the explorer who shares something of Frankenstein's ambitious nature, discovers the monster hanging over the dead body of the emaciated scientist he had rescued from the cold polar waters:

Over him hung a form which I cannot find words to describe; gigantic in stature, yet uncouth and distorted in its proportions. As he hung over the coffin, his face was concealed by long locks of ragged hair; but one vast hand was extended, in colour and apparent texture like that of a mummy. When he heard the sound of my approach, he ceased to utter exclamations of grief and horror, and sprung towards the window. (*F*.218)

Gothic alienation serves as the vehicle for the poignant discrepancy between emotion and physical appearance. The suffering of the monster who has murdered its creator is sharply at odds with the hideous, 'loathsome' appearance it presents to Walton. Its 'wild and incoherent self-reproaches' pinpoint the pain of a life determined by a previously inconceivable orphancy and reveal the rage and self-hatred that can befall a victim of injustice. (*F*.219) Forced right from its inception into a posture of marginality, its heightened visibility hurts it more than words can convey. The creature bit by bit is forced to discover itself as a monster: its being for itself determined by the gaze of others. It is as if Rousseau's little girl had kept writing, kept staring at herself in the mirror.

Early on in the narrative the monster repeats the mythic posture of Narcissus, but with radically disparate results. In the pool of water, it discovers its own image. But instead of a figure so enticing that consciousness longs to fuse with it, desire drawn into its own uncanny web, the creature draws back in sheer revulsion, unable to separate its sense of its physical body, reflected in the still waters, from the horror that others attach to it. Consciousness succumbs to a bodily being already defined as a 'miserable deformity'. At first in all too human fashion, the creature refuses to accept the mirror image. Then filled with 'the bitterest sensations of despondence and mortification', it is convinced of the truth: 'that I was in reality the monster that I am.' (*F*.114) And so begins one of the most painful of Romantic educations, one that only a woman, a slave or a colonised subject could imagine.

In a world where to appear, was to exist for the gaze,

the woman writer found her own intimate self cut away from the clasp of self-consciousness, her feminine being alienated. It was a condition that Mary Shelley fleshed out in her symbolic use of the grotesque, the monster's physicality violating the requirements of beauty, its hideous embodiment corroding the cultural prescriptions for the feminine. Yet by acting as a negativity to the accepted forms of social interaction, the monstrous being reveals the injustice on which human order is built. Indeed this darker, more ferocious message in Mary Shelley's text, undercuts the more easily assimilable notion that by leaving behind the realms of shared love and conjugality, the world of the feminine and family bonds, Victor perverted the 'natural' form that life might have taken. Theodor Adorno stated the problem:

> The feminine character, and the ideal of femininity on which it is modelled, are products of masculine society. The image of undistorted nature arises only in distortion, as its opposite. Where it claims to be humane, masculine society imperiously breeds in woman its own corrective, and shows itself through this limitation implacably the master. The feminine character is a negative imprint of domination.[4]

Mortal Birth

'I collected bones from charnel-houses; and disturbed, with profane fingers, the tremendous secrets of the human frame', confesses Victor Frankenstein. In his 'workshop of filthy creation' he begins to put together what he conceives of as a super-human body. (*F*.54-55) But there is a radical discrepancy between the stuff that he manipulates with his fingers, the dead matter that he struggles to refashion and reanimate, and the workings of his isolate Romantic will. It is as if the *res cogitans* and the *res extensa*, the phenomena of mind and body that Descartes had so much trouble holding together in his grand, solitary meditations on knowledge and existence, had split apart yet again, now in a chilling Gothic format. The ugliness of the monster serves to emphasise its irreducible physicality. Scarred and stuck together in dismal disproportion, its appearance parodies stereotypes of feminine beauty or virile masculinity. It was Mary Shelley's genius not to stop at the mere surfaces of things, but to give the monster a needy, questing soul. And what the creature longs for are precisely those bonds of family and compassionate love that Victor cast aside in his quest for immortality and power.

A mother's counsel to her infant daughter in Wollstone-craft's *Maria*, 'always appear what you are', harkens back to an earlier age of Romantic belief, when astute, impassioned writers actually believed that the shared world might be remade through the powers of visionary perception. But what can it mean for Mary Shelley's monster to appear as he is? Maria's counsel is impossible to fulfil. Given the fearful, suspicious nature of human beings, the creature has no way of mediating what is within with what is outside himself. Or rather, the old Romantic terms of inside and outside collapse when not held together by a human body of acceptable appearance. In her mother's world, a woman had to struggle for visible power, for a truth that would not be rationed off according to sex.

In Mary Shelley's world a dark irony illuminates the very terms of the existential proposition: 'always appear what you are'. The monster discovers that to others he is all body. By virtue of his body he is radically displaced. There is literally nowhere he can be. The phenomenological connection forged by the woman writer between appearance and existence, between spatial existence and being for the other, takes on a ferocious enactment. Female Romanticism, as it passes from mother to daughter, sets up a powerful stream of subversive knowledge, pondering, questioning, overturning the Romantic vision of epistemological perfectibility.

But there was tragedy incipient in this knowledge, which is perhaps why it has been so hard to make a tradition out of these passages between mother and daughter. For the sources of Mary Shelley's creativity cannot be severed from the trauma of birth. The awareness that her mother, a famous and to many an infamous woman of letters, died giving birth to her, fused with the numbing pain of infant mortality. Three out of Mary Shelley's own four children either died in infancy or earliest childhood, leaving the young Mary with a permanent weakened sense of being, an ontological insecurity so radical that it could only be validated in creative terms by a palpable outrage at the fact of being born. Thus embodiment itself becomes cause for rage, the human creature's helplessness and vulnerability, reaping power and with it the permission to a passionate symbolism through revolt.

Dorothy Dinnerstein argues that the individuating consciousness identifies the mother – she out of whose flesh it has come – as intrinsic part of nature, of the pre-given context. As such the mother is often taken to be constricting, part of things as they are, the old world that must be broken open. The evolving self conceives of the maternal in terms of an irreducible antagonism. For Dinnerstein, this antagonism, which spills over into the general view of women, can only be overcome if the nurture of children is shared between men and women: 'It is true then', she writes, 'that we are born mortal and born of woman . . . Woman is now the focus of our ambivalence to the flesh.'[5]

In Mary Shelley this discomfort at embodiment finds its focus in the problem of physical existence: its gestation and ensoulment, death and the corruption of flesh. In her work the very fact of being in a body, of having a body, is laid open to question, subject to a scrutiny and an outrage almost without parallel in the Romantic era.

It is only in her precursor Blake that one discovers an adequate Romantic counterpart to Mary Shelley's ferocious questioning of bodily being. Blake's radical humanism led him to a vision of embodiment that celebrated energy, sexuality and the forces of desire, subverting the old Cartesian notion of a superior reason and inferior animal substance. The voice of the Devil in his *Marriage of Heaven and Hell* (1793), after setting out the conventional wisdom that there are two principles, Body and Soul, reverses that received knowledge, arguing for the Body as merely 'a portion of Soul discerned by the five Senses, the chief inlets of Soul in this age.' Thus energy and with it, sexual passion become the life of the body – true source of imaginative knowledge – and reason, once held to be the vehicle of truth is revealed as nothing other than the 'bound or outward circumference of Energy' – its stopping place, its rim of exhaustion.

Yet there are cracks in Blake's vision of embodiment as an imaginative source. A battle breaks out, a mutilation at the heart of bodily being. 'To Tirzah' (c. 1802), a four stanza poem added to later versions of *The Songs of Innocence and Experience*, presents a speaker haunted by 'Mortal Birth'. To be born is to be betrayed into death. Bodily being stands for a closure of spiritual existence, a crossing out of immortality. The cruelty of maternity follows on. The speaker must fight Tirzah, 'Mother of my mortal part'. The poet's ongoing struggle with the order of things, with oppression deeply rooted both in society and within the human psyche, has extended itself to maternity, the genesis of being-in-a-body.

Misogyny both literal and symbolic translates the outrage of birth: for to be born is also to fall into sexual distinction, into division, into death. 'Generation', the act of sexual reproduction and its accompanying cycle of birth and death, must be broken. In the design that accompanies the poem

Blake inscribed a line from the Bible: 'It is raised a spiritual
body.' The citation from 1 Corinthians 15:44 underlines the
bitterness at the fleshly 'Mother' whose very substance as
portion of nature, cannot be sloughed away. In an implicit
deployment of the Romantic trope that identifies woman
with nature and its materiality, Blake's speaker struggles
to free himself:

> Thou Mother of my Mortal part
> With cruelty didst mould my Heart,
> And with false self-deceiving tears,
> Didst bind my Nostrils, Eyes and Ears
> Didst close my Tongue in senseless clay
> And me to Mortal life betray . . . (*B*.30)

When the Mother betrays, who can save? The great cry
from the Preludium to *Europe A Prophecy* (1794) springs
to mind: 'Then why shouldst thou accursed mother bring
me into life?' (*B*.59) Cut from the 'sensual enjoyment' of a
soul and body well united, life is nothing but constriction.
Clearly in 'To Tirzah' the revolutionary fervour so characteristic of Blake, has turned tail, consuming itself in rage at
bodily birth, a fact that the imagination which had sought
to recreate heaven and earth cannot overcome. And the
mother as source of the fleshly body absorbs the brunt of
anger.

In his Ode, 'Intimations of Immortality from Recollections of Early Childhood' (composed 1802-4; published
1807), Wordsworth speaks of the 'prison house' of ordinary
bodily life that closes around the growing child. While
custom and ceremony, the human realms of do and don't
work their vengeance on the child's soul, Wordsworth's
vision at least in that poem, is able to conceive of birth
itself as a 'sleep and a forgetting', capable of redeeming
itself to the extent that some memory of pre-existence is
still possible. The Wordsworthian mode is characteristically

elegiac. In Blake there is outrage and revolt. No recompense is possible and none is sought from the 'Mother of my Mortal part'. Nothing that is, except total liberation from her. While a man might make such a passionate claim, even while recognising its ultimate impossibility, at least where origins are at stake, for a woman however compulsive her need, such a liberation, if that is the appropriate word, can only lead into nihilism.

Unstable Substances (*Frankenstein* and 'Transformation')

The night he finally has seen his creature breathe, a moment that had required a relentless, cruel hunt for the secrets of life, Victor Frankenstein tries desperately to sleep, to escape from the disgust that a deformed conception inspires in him. Exhausted by the intensity of a repulsion that equals only 'the beauty of the dream' he is overwhelmed in sleep by a dream so vivid that it usurps whatever territory his ordinary life might have carved out for itself. (*F*.57) It is a dream of sexual longing turned to feverish guilt, of maternal death, decay and corruption. Behind Elizabeth Lavenza, his adopted sister and beloved, lies the figure of a mother, Caroline Beaufort, who had died of scarlet fever contracted when she nursed the young girl back to health. The carnal embrace split by the image of a dead mother reveals the terror that lies at the heart of Mary Shelley's play with substances, a play that touches both literary creation and female procreation:

I thought I saw Elizabeth, in the bloom of health, walking in the streets of Ingolstadt. Delighted and surprised, I embraced her; but as I imprinted the first kiss on her lips, they became livid with the hue of death; her features appeared to change and I thought that I held the corpse of my dead mother in my arms; a shroud enveloped her form, and I saw the grave-worms crawling in the folds of the flannel. (*F*.58)

Femininity has sought and found its own nemesis. If, as Harold Bloom argues, the male poet was haunted by the power of a precursor he had to struggle with and overthrow, the woman writer focusing on creation itself, discovers in the darkness of her physicality, sources of terror that no images of rebirth or recreation can adequately absolve.[6] The glorious obsession of the young man, inspired at the very start by the destruction incipient in nature itself – the bolt of lightning that shredded the great oak – turns through the displacements of symbolic language into a medium fit for a young woman's pain.

It is impossible for me to read these lines on Victor's dream and not think of Mary Shelley, her consciousness haunted by the maternal death her own being had unwittingly caused, her sense of sexual fervour undercut by the fact of mortality. What would it be like, I have often asked myself while reading Mary Shelley, to know that your mother died giving birth to you? What would it be like to feel that the very source of life was invaded by death?

Not only did her own mother die eleven days after she was born, but the young Mary who had eloped with the brilliant, wayward poet Percy Bysshe Shelley, found herself pregnant at the age of sixteen. In Mary Shelley's journal, the birth of her first child is recorded in Shelley's hand. The young mother nursed her firstborn, and the sudden access of health in both mother and child was noted by Shelley in an entry for February 25: 'The child very well; Maie very well also; drawing milk all day.'

For her part Mary records the following day how she read Mme de Staël's *Corinne*, how she conversed with Hogg, how she nursed her baby. The entry for March 1 repeats the basic routine, the brief burst of historical awareness – 'Bonaparte invades France' – absorbed into the rush of domestic life, the new baby, the facts of moving house. The abrupt, yet oddly reassuring sentences, the rhythm of reading and nursing – mind and body both functioning extraordinarily well in the aftermath of childbirth – fractures suddenly with the pitiful entry for March 6, the brevity of the sentences unchanged, yet forced to bear burden of death, of a mother's grief that has little outlet. The slightly sinister book she was reading, the comforting presence of Hogg, both mask over the despair that would soon overwhelm her:

> Thursday, Mar.9. – Read and talk. Still think about my little baby – 'tis hard, indeed, for a mother to lose a child . . .
>
> Monday Mar.13. – Shelley and Clara go to town. Stay at home; net, and think of my little dead baby. This is foolish, I suppose; yet, whenever I am left alone to my own thoughts, and do not read to divert them, they always come back to the same point – that I was a mother and am so no longer . . .
>
> Sunday Mar.19. Dream that my little baby came to life again; that it had only been cold, and that we rubbed it before the fire, and it lived. Awake and find no baby. I think about the little thing all day. Not in good spirits . . . (*MSJ*.40-41)

In January 1816, the following year, Mary gave birth to her son William, and in June that summer she began work on her novel *Frankenstein*. The obsession with creating life where death had forever altered it, with passing through the 'ideal bounds' of life and death, become part of Victor's character. (*F*.54) The young man wants nothing so much as to be 'capable of bestowing animation upon lifeless matter.' (*F*.52) By turning Victor's magnificent obsession into a substantial horror, the young woman may be seen as teaching herself a humility in the face of immobilising circumstances, accepting the limits of birth and death. But the outrage at the monster's humiliation is too palpable for easy reconciliation, and the murders that fill the text, even if dictated by the unfolding of a Gothic structure, too vivid for simple appeasement.

In his Preface to *The Cenci* (1819), Shelley wrote of the horror of incest and rape that Beatrice Cenci had to undergo, her implication in the murder of her cruel father, her subsequent imprisonment and execution:

> The story of the Cenci is indeed eminently fearful and monstrous . . . The person who would treat such a subject must increase the ideal, and diminish the actual horror of the events . . . The highest moral purpose aimed at in the highest species of drama, is the teaching the human heart, through its sympathies and antipathies, the knowledge of itself. (*S*.239-40)

To teach the human heart, 'the knowledge of itself' is a fitting aim for a poet. But while Percy held tight to his vision of spiritual redemption through self-knowledge – 'in proportion to the possession of which knowledge, every human being is wise, just, sincere, tolerant and kind' – for Mary, such knowledge brought little forgiveness. To a woman whose mother had died in order to give her birth, whose own experiences of childbirth and childrearing were fraught with anguish, the grounds of life itself seemed cause for grievance.

Anne Mellor in her recent study argues that in the 1831 edition of *Frankenstein* (the text I have used for this study is based on the 1831 edition) Mary Shelley moves closer to a darker, more fatalistic vision of nature and leaves far less scope for human agency. Her revisions of the novel heighten the sense of natural laws working themselves out, 'inexorable, beyond human control.' Mellor sees Victor as turned into more a victim of bad influence than an overreacher, brought low by his own moral culpability so that 'Imperial nature, the substance itself' can triumph.[7] Mellor's insights work well with an analysis of Mary Shelley's struggle with chaos, and the substantial basis of life.

In the 1831 introduction to *Frankenstein* Mary Shelley ponders the question of origins:

Everything must have a beginning . . . and that beginning must be linked to something that went before . . . Invention, it must be humbly admitted, does not consist in creating out of void, but out of chaos; the materials must, in the first place be afforded: it can give form to dark, shapeless substances, but cannot bring into being the substance itself. (*F*.8)

For Mary Shelley, the roots of a Romantic mythology lay not in intense, metaphysical claims about the powers of human consciousness and its sublime capacities, but in a return to the very substances of being, the flesh which we are. Time and again we find that the critical imaginative task for her was to rework that 'dark, shapeless' ground of origin, struggling to make sense of the disappearance of life, of the corruption of human substance. In so doing, she links power to deformity and the feminine to a pale, unequal beauty, its forced compliance to the order of things highlighting the coarse, the vulgar and the ambitious. Yet power – cleft from the feminine – even as it is frequently stamped by ugliness or deformity, is weakened by its bond with flesh and matter.

The source of the grotesque, Wolfgang Kayser has argued in his study of the subject, is not primarily the problem of individual action or the destruction of moral order. Rather, in terms directly relevant to our reflection on Mary Shelley, he sees in the grotesque 'the expression of our failure to orient ourselves in the physical universe.'[8]

The phrase has a peculiar resonance for women writers, who must travel backwards in their quest for an origin, recognising their own bodies as the source of imaginative life, reaping with this knowledge all the ambivalence that flesh is heir to.

*   *   *

There are times when Mary Shelley plays fast and loose with the stuff of physical being, redeeming what she cannot alter. The boundaries of self-identity, instead of being caught and wrapped up in a single body, are traded back and forth between the visible and ordinary and the invisible and extraordinary, with no clear lines of transaction laid down. Indeed the commerce between bodies is fraught with uncertainty and is often the cause of death, as we see in the monstrous flesh of Frankenstein's creation, or the tiny, contorted dwarf of her short story 'Transformation' (1830), hideous but magical, splitting apart spirit and matter, will and necessity, desire and its bitter fulfilment.

In 'Transformation' handsome young Guido, spendthrift, profligate, every inch the rake, is cast out from his native Genoa. In order to return and claim the virtuous, beautiful Juliet whom he could never deserve, he exchanges his body with a dwarf. In return he receives the dwarf's sea-chest filled with 'blazing jewels'. The narrative makes clear that such transubstantiations are part and parcel of a fallen world. The dwarf claims the frightened fascinated young man as a fellow being, a 'cousin of Lucifer', consumed by overweening pride. Guido in turn, urged on to revenge and violent abduction by the dwarf, finds himself unable to turn away from naked power: 'It was tempting Providence to interchange talk with this magician. But *Power*, in all its shapes, is venerable to man.'[9] Indeed the dwarf could not be uglier. Cast up from the ocean like some primitive beast, he seems scarcely human and there is nothing in the perceiving consciousness to transform him into the instrument of apt learning.

The old man in Wordsworth's 'Resolution and Independence', first seen as a huge stone or sea-beast, bit by bit becomes the visionary source of endurance and stoical piety. Mary Shelley's dwarf, however, cannot be transformed by visionary knowledge. It retains a stubborn form. The misshapen body is left with Guido, and the dwarf's consciousness in the handsome body steals into Juliet's chamber to seduce her. Just in the nick of time, the deformed embodiment stumbles in. In the fight till death the two bloods mingle for an instant, just as the dwarf had urged Guido. Weakened but victorious, Guido watches the dwarf die, and enters then into his own body. Now he is able to claim Juliet. He sets himself up in grand style. He falls in love with mirrors, surrounding himself with them so that his body just regained may be on constant display: self returned to body in the restitution of narcissistic desire.

There is no obvious moral to the story. Guido is not better, not sadder or wiser, at least not in any self evident manner. His adventure is not overtly didactic. The monstrous encounter however, clarifies the nature of desire, grants a knowledge that Guido himself in large part is exempt from. Contemplating the dwarf before they had exchanged bodies, Guido asked:

A human being bestriding a sea-chest! – A human being! – Yet was it one? Surely never such had existed before – a misshapen dwarf with squinting eyes, distorted features, and body deformed . . . But *Power*, in all its shapes, is venerable to man. (*CT*.127-8)

Guido is transfixed, filled with a 'clinging fascination' and cannot turn back. When he takes on the dwarf body he gains a knowledge that physical beauty had kept from him. In his deformed, degraded embodiment he cowers from the fishermen's huts on the shore fearful that even the boys might stone him to death. However there is nothing at the end, when he stands surrounded by his mirrors to indicate that he has gained in moral insight. As in *Frankenstein*, the twinned selves are linked in fierce, addictive need, then consumed finally in oblivion. The return of the repressed, entails destruction. Doubling and splitting minds and bodies Mary Shelley plays with self-identity and power, themes that haunted the Romantics, though her play is seldom in jest and the odds sometimes too terrible to countenance.

The Case of Justine

Frankenstein's monster is no aberration. In symbolic terms its bodily being is an utter necessity, casting into relief the difficult truth about embodied selves. While Victor delves into the secrets of nature, he loses a shared family life. The obsession that turns his spirit into its own enemy is played out in detail, with the lovely, ultimately helpless Elizabeth Lavenza as his good angel. However the schematic morality that seems implicit in the novel breaks down precisely because the monster and its creator are twinned and doubled till one cannot tell itself apart from the other. 'My own vampire, my own spirit let loose from the grave, and forced to destroy all that was dear to me', cries out Victor in a sudden shock of recognition. He has glimpsed the forbidden truth: the monster has murdered his little brother William.

The name William bears pondering. It was Godwin's name, the beloved father to whom Mary dedicated this first book. It was the name she had given her son, her second child to whom she was deeply attached, born to her in January 1816, six months before she began work on *Frankenstein*. It was also the name of the imaginary child invoked by her dead mother Mary Wollstonecraft in her fragmentary *Lessons* (1797), the boy child she thought she was carrying, the pregnant woman blind, as one necessarily is, to the being within her. Mary Wollstonecraft's maternal desire for a male child, to be named after Godwin, works its way into the figure of the beautiful boy choked to death on the mountain slope. Instants before he is murdered, William struggles violently, crying 'Hideous monster! Let me go. My papa is a Syndic – he is M. Frankenstein – he will punish you'. The monster stops, drawn to a pendant the child wears around his neck, 'a portrait of a most lovely woman.' (*F*.142) It was the image of Caroline, mother of both Victor and William. The monster is delighted by her lashes and lips, the serene and lovely expression on her face. But he draws back sharply, realising that the woman, had she lived and seen him, could only have been repulsed by his flagrant, misshapen body. He tears the locket off the dead child and hides it in the clothes of the sleeping Justine. It is Justine, innocent and helpless, who will pay for the murder.

If in Mary Shelley's finest work there is a measure of transcendence, it lies in the courage that drew her forward to symbolise, imagining a realm of absolute will power and in its train, self-conscious yet helpless destruction, the ruin of the good. Keeping herself apart as best she could from the molten stuff of her own imagination, she carved out her women characters by and large as imprints of a culturally sanctioned femininity, lovely, nurturing and ultimately helpless. Yet the bonds of femininity clarify the evil that time and again humiliates the good, deforms or destroys the life-giving impulses. Through the fate of the feminine, the radical instability of the realm of appearances is cast into relief.

The case of Justine in the novel *Frankenstein* provides an exemplification. Who is Justine? Why is she in the novel? How is she relevant to the struggle between Victor and his monster? The slippery nature of what passes for knowledge in a world where little is certain, least of all justice, emerges most clearly in the trial and conviction of the innocent maid-servant Justine. 'She was warmly attached to the child now dead, and acted to him like a most affectionate mother', says Elizabeth Lavenza speaking out at Justine's trial. (*F*.84-5)

But the young woman, sensing the hatred of the public and fearful that the machinery of the law will convict her, confesses to her guilt. It is a false confession, the tormented Justine explains to Elizabeth and Victor who visit her in prison for the last time, voiced in the hopes of escaping the hell fire her confessor had threatened her with, his image of the hereafter overcoming her fragile, anguished innocence: 'I did confess but I confessed a lie . . . my confessor has besieged me; he threatened and menaced, until I almost began to think that I was the monster that he said I was.' (*F*.87) There is no escape. Justine dies, and Victor who knows full well that his creature is the true murderer, says nothing, his silence sealing his unwritten pact with the nameless, grotesque being he has made and abandoned. 'I bore a hell within me which nothing could extinguish', he confesses, absolving himself even as he absorbs the destructive powers of the monster. He sees in the dead William and Justine 'the first hapless victims of my unhallowed arts.' (*F*.89)

For Mary Shelley, the world as it is besieges the innocent, and crushes the sense of justice within the individual self. Justine discarded as a child by her own mother, bewildered and confused by her intrinsic innocence, cannot withstand the force of her accusers. Victor, the only one who might have stepped forward to help her, refuses to do so. His explanation that he would be taken for a madman merely covers up his deepest fidelity – to the monster he has created. Things are not what they seem, the realm of appearance is fatally flawed.

In October 1822, a little over three months after Shelley's death, Mary, engrossed in her pain, notes the disparity between the '*internal* life' that she leads and the 'outward and apparent one'. She tells of the seemingly smooth surface of her life disturbed by an undercurrent that 'distorts all objects reflected in it'. She moves on to an implicit acknowledgement of the symbolic worlds she has created: 'the mind is no longer a mirror in which outward events may reflect themselves, but becomes itself the painter and creator.' (*MSJ*.183) While clearly a reflection of the intensity of grief, her statement has a relevance for all of her life as a writing woman. The depths within consciousness disturb and distort a public existence the feminine self could neither wholly acknowledge nor wholly sever itself from.

The cleavage between inwardness and the outer world, so critical for Romantics, had been mediated for Mary Wollstonecraft by the integrity of the feminine self, by the quest for a truth that in the final analysis would never betray consciousness. Her revolutionary impulse was never to leave her, the belief in the world to be remade, necessary to the sorts of didacticism that she pledged herself to. For her daughter, however, the world was a much more unstable place, and truth if glimpsed, adhered to nothing that was not conceived of and borne within the inwardness. But the inwardness in turn was radically cleft, its self-division a function both of the scepticism that invaded the second generation of Romantics and the condition of a woman writer who knew the cost that publicity and worldly power could exact. Truth then could rarely enter the public world and monstrousness, even as it signified distortion and deformity, stood for things in themselves, grotesque, unvarnished yet pierced by a Romantic longing.

Wollstonecraft's sense of the monstrous, in marked contrast, always had a clear moral basis to it. 'I recognised her pale visage; I listened to the tale told by the spectators, and my heart did not burst. I thought of my own state and wondered how I could be such a monster! . . . ' (*MWW*.116) These words are spoken not by Victor Frankenstein, or the monster he has created, but by Jemima, the warder in the prison into which Maria, heroine of Wollstonecraft's unfinished novel, was flung. Jemima tells her tale while recognising her implicit cruelty. In her jealousy she has driven a pregnant woman to suicide by persuading her lover to throw her out of doors. Her recognition of guilt, her awareness of a shared fate with the dead woman, drives Jemima forward till in the prison house, coming upon the passionate Maria, she is able to turn to her in friendship till the two of them escape, their sense of justice permitting them to survive a world whose insanity turns women into outlaws.

To instruct others, particularly other women, presupposes a bond of experience, a veracity of knowledge that can be passed on, a sense that the intimate self however betrayed by the state of the social world is part and parcel of a finer order, a world that must be brought into being through mental labour. To be a mother, however fraught with anguish, is to be part of the future. Indeed Maria still in prison is able to tell her story precisely because the new life of her daughter, a life in which she has invested so much faith, might still persist, somehow, somewhere, unknown to her. Overt didacticism was no part of Mary Shelley's aim. Nor was the revolutionary quest for a finer, future order something she could contemplate without a painful, and even embittering irony.

7 Revising the Feminine

Lucy in Goslar

Wordsworth's tender, elegiac 'Lucy' poems (five were composed 1798-9), published in 1800; one 'I travelled among unknown men' was composed in 1801 and published much later in 1807) have long been the subject of critical interest. Each evokes a feminine figure. Whether adult or child, named or nameless, she is bound to the natural landscape. She crystallises loss, intense longing. She is the impossible object of the poet's desire, an iconic representation of the Romantic feminine. Both Dorothy Wordsworth and Mary Shelley knew the poems. While Dorothy read and copied them out from the earliest versions onwards, Mary Shelley read them across a gulf of time. The first Romantics were still alive, but that way of life, those revolutionary aspirations had vanished. As late as her novel *The Last Man* (1826), Wordsworth's Lucy provided Mary Shelley with a way of reading, and revising, the Romantic vision of femininity.

'She dwelt among the untrodden ways' was of special interest to both Dorothy Wordsworth and Mary Shelley. The figure of a veiled and modest Lucy, her very being dependent on the intensity of the poet's gaze, provided these women readers with an intimate image of what femininity might be like, if it were predicated upon Romantic vision.

In December 1789, when William and Dorothy Wordsworth were living in Goslar, enduring as best they could the

hardship of a German winter, they addressed a joint letter
to Coleridge who had travelled with them from England.
Coleridge was in Ratzeburg, improving his German and
studying the philosophers. In the letter Dorothy transcribed
an early version of 'She dwelt among the untrodden ways'.
The final version opens with a remote, natural landscape
that harbours the reclusive Lucy, her modesty and loveliness imaged in violet and star. The early draft that Dorothy
copied out opens with the stock image of a woman with lips
as red as roses. It is tonally strident, lacking the delicate
refinement so characteristic of the 'Lucy' poems:

> My hope was one, from cities far,
> Nursed on a lonesome heath;
> Her lips were red as roses are,
> Her hair a woodbine wreath. (*EY*.236)

What does it mean to invoke as one's 'hope' a woman
whose whole life was lived out as a lingering, unreal
existence 'dead to the world'? The fourth stanza makes
clear she suffered a 'slow distemper' that infected her flesh,
preventing fruitfulness. She died on the very heath where
she was 'nursed'. Who nursed her? The question hangs in
the air. Any maternal figure that might have been, blurs
into the natural landscape.

The third and loveliest stanza (preserved intact as
the central stanza in the final version), celebrates the
tenderness of her flesh, its very fragility heightened
when set by the unmoving stone, and then her flickering visibility picked out in the image of the solitary
star:

> A violet by a mossy stone
> Half hidden from the eye!
> Fair as a star, when only one
> Is shining in the sky! (*EY*.237/*PW*.2:30)

By virtue of the speaker's love, she exists. Her literal death and the 'difference' it makes for the lover heightens the power of his vision. Her gradual vanishing intensifies the value of his consciousness. The beloved woman suffers a double absorption: into nature and into the male speaker's imagination. Now she can be magnified without fixed boundaries and stand as a symbol for the impossibility of fulfilled desire. The 'Lucy' poems exemplify what Sartre said of Proust: 'a Spider-Spirit that draws things into its web . . . slowly digests them, reduces them to itself.'[1]

Coleridge was the first of a long line of readers to sense in the 'Lucy' poems Wordsworth's deep buried passion for his sister Dorothy. In a letter of April 6, 1799, he writes of 'A Slumber Did My Spirit Seal', which he had just received from Goslar, as 'a most sublime Epitaph'. 'Most probably, in some gloomier moment he [Wordsworth] had fancied the moment in which his Sister might die.' (*CL*.I:274) More recently, F.W. Bateson unleashed a protracted controversy by arguing that Wordsworth could not have survived with his mind intact except by disposing of his feelings for Dorothy as expressed in the 'Lucy' poems: 'The dangerous relationship with Dorothy was now solved, subconsciously, by killing her off symbolically.'[2]

Dorothy herself had strong feelings towards the poems that she transcribed. After copying the early version of 'She dwelt among untrodden ways', she jots down a single line as a textual fence to separate herself from the feminine image of the poem: 'The next poem is a favourite of mine i.e. of me Dorothy'. Yet by naming herself ('me Dorothy'), she reinforces a sense of her own autonomy, distinct from the fate of the vanishing beloved in the poem she has just transcribed.

She much prefers the life and vitality of the second Lucy, secure in her cottage on the hill, its walls marking her off from the natural surroundings. At the close of that poem (an early, striking version of 'Strange fits of passion have I known') the woman turns back at the poet, taunting him with her laughter as he confides in her his sudden, inexplicable dream of her death. In this second 'Lucy' poem the beloved is at the height of her powers. She is 'strong and gay', a rose in the full blush of summer. In contrast, the poet, his bodily vitality weakened by dream, is 'bent' and must force his way uphill towards her. Rhythmically, monotonously, 'hoof after hoof' his horse picks its way towards the woman's cottage. The speaker fixes his eye on the moon. Suddenly the moon falls behind the cottage roof and the dream fails.

The sheer solidity of Lucy's house, a figuration surely of her body, blocks the poet's gaze. Is it in 'self-defence', William's phrase in this joint letter, that the speaker invokes another dream, fiercer than the first? But while in the finished draft, the fear that Lucy might indeed be dead, is left to conclude the poem, in this early version of the poem that Dorothy delighted in, the woman's voice turns on the speaker as he confesses his fears:

> I told her this; her laughter light
> Is ringing in my ears;
> And when I think upon that night
> My eyes are dim with tears. (*EY*.238)

Dorothy's response is compelling, not just for what it reveals about her as a reader of her brother's poetry, but also for the glimpse into her obsession with the problem of being housed, the woman's fragile sense of selfhood bound up, often in quite complicated ways, with the substances of the surrounding world, both natural and man-made. However intensely she felt about her bond with her brother and her role as helpmate, she retained a vivid sense of her own needs.

Dorothy's 'Thoughts on my sick-bed'

Death, disease and the suffering consciousness are all themes relevant to Dorothy Wordsworth's poem 'Thoughts on my sick-bed', a late poem in which she responds quite directly to her brother's celebrated 'Tintern Abbey'. In 'Tintern Abbey' Dorothy's figure enters in at the very end, her presence a response to the pressure of mortality. Her voice, the 'shooting lights' of her 'wild eyes' are evoked by Wordsworth as a stay against his own inevitable dissolution. Her female body, by retrieving all the intensity of a past self, becomes an icon of powers he has lost. And so without discomfort he can imagine her, a beloved double to his own self, recapturing his world through their twinned gazes, her future weighted down with the burden of his most precious past:

> . . . . Nor, perchance,
> If I should be, where I no more can hear
> Thy voice, nor catch from thy wild eyes these gleams
> Of past existence, wilt thou then forget
> That on the banks of this delightful stream
> We stood together . . . (*PW*.2:263)

The poem was to haunt her. Years later, bedridden, her sense of past mobility a painful memory at best, she evokes her brother's vision of her, a vision now of lost being, her body utterly immobile, the very antitype in sickness and incipient madness to that of the quick young woman who walked with her brother into the Wye Valley.[3] In 'Thoughts on my sick-bed' she perfects, if in dark, disturbing fashion, the posture of a femininity that had acquiesced to its own absorption into genius. Shorn of her mobility and the moving, almost febrile sense of self it had permitted her, she writes from within his text. William becomes more completely than ever before, the site where she must seek her vindication. In her poem, his image-making powers are celebrated in a touching, shared triumph, her existence in the lonely room illumined by the perpetual elsewhere his poem provides her with. Her pain, her loss of the ordinary pleasures, her crippled body are justified in the momentary glory of their shared existences, parallel lives that having lost each other, must converge again in the words of a poem:

> No prisoner in this lonely room,
> I *saw* the green banks of the Wye,
> Recalling thy prophetic words,
> Bard, Brother, Friend from infancy!
>
> (*DC.MS.120.59v*)

In turning to 'Tintern Abbey' she is maintaining a poetic strategy set up earlier in this poem, when she directly evokes a 'Lucy' poem 'She dwelt among the untrodden ways'.

Dorothy harkens back to her brother's 'violet by a mossy stone' and reviews it from a woman's perspective. She takes the fictive violet and refigures its meaning. It becomes 'The violet betrayed by its noiseless breath'.

How are we to make sense of this line? Her violet is doubly betrayed: first it is rendered perceptible – hence betrayed – in the very act of breathing. Yet if it were not to breathe how could it live? Secondly it is betrayed, in and for itself, by its intense privacy.

The lines might be read in much more cheerful fashion, in a manner consonant with the previous image of the 'silent butterfly spreading its wings', or the subsequent image of a 'daffodil dancing in the breeze'. All three are natural objects that have given themselves up to the speaker's 'busy eyes'.

Still I cannot help reading in the violet, a charged intimacy, a femininity the other images lack, personal associations brought to the fore in a poignant self-definition through negativity:

> No need of motion, or of strength,
> Or even the breathing air:
> I thought of Nature's loveliest scenes;
> And with memory I was there. (*DC.MS*.120 59v)

In almost fatal formation, the quick of life circling back to the image, Dorothy approaches the symbolic stasis her brother valued so deeply, an 'amphibious' state that renders the object most capable of assimilation into the Wordsworthian consciousness. The appetitive consciousness of Romanticism has here achieved its feminine complement. That these lines were penned by Dorothy on her sickbed, while the brilliant, quick-silver genius of her earlier self could evade all such formulations, should only alert us to the incurable danger of power that is released by drawing oneself through the very eye of desire.

* * *

There is a poignant tale to the reading of 'Tintern Abbey' and its intense hold on the imaginations of both brother and sister. In a letter of September 1848, half a century after the poem was composed and more than a decade and a half after Dorothy's 'Thoughts on my sick-bed', the Duke of Argyle tells of visiting Rydal Mount. Wordsworth, an old man now, read out 'Tintern Abbey' in a fervent voice that his listener found 'very striking and beautiful'. While noting that Mary Wordsworth was deeply moved by the reading, the listener finds himself somewhat uncomfortable in the presence of an intensity 'almost unnatural' when the poet read out the lines addressed to his sister Dorothy. Only later, with a sharp pang does the honourable visitor realise that the words 'My dear, *dear* friend' and 'in thy wild eyes' referred to 'the old paralytic and *doited* woman' he had seen earlier. The terrible pity of it all strikes him: 'It was melancholy to think that the vacant silly stare which we had seen in the morning was from the 'wild eyes' of 1798.'[4]

In the years of her 'madness', Dorothy had bouts of ferocious behaviour, striking the faces and arms of those who took care of her. Mary Wordsworth describes a restlessness that sometimes turned violent, the short lived gleams of intelligence in her stricken sister-in-law, an intense preoccupation with her own self and her own feelings, so markedly in contrast with Dorothy's earlier self: 'Her restless feelings (which we attribute to something amiss going on in the head, which she rubs perpetually), prevent her finding quiet from reading – nor will she often *listen* to it. She says "she is too busy with her own feelings" . . . Her greatest discomforts proceed from habits I cannot describe – and it would be painful to us both were I to attempt it.'[5]

How are we to interpret Dorothy's behaviour? She herself in a time of lucidity, in a letter of 1836 to her nephew Christopher describes the 'torn caps of my nurses and the heavy blows I have given their heads and faces'. Her 'mighty struggle' is painful to ponder. (*LY*.3:198) Is it possible to read this spurt of violence as the surfacing of power repressed by years of modest, circumspect living, years in which she was accountable to all others, her brother, her sister-in-law, their children and friends? It is hard to tell. Too clear cut a reading could shear away the complexities of life lived, ignore facts we can only guess at. What seems to be the case however is that Dorothy, immobile now, after her years of swift, vital movement, gains a power over those around her. And this power, passionate power, is a deformity, a contortion of what ought to be. Speculating now that her mental disturbances had a root in her emotive life, rather than in any physical or chemical imbalance, we can say with clarity, but without absolute certainty that she should not have had to mortgage her sanity in order to gain her rights as a poet.

Femininity and Betrayal (*The Last Man*)

Almost three decades after Dorothy Wordsworth transcribed the earliest drafts of two of her brother's 'Lucy' poems, Mary Shelley published her novel *The Last Man* (1826). The novel was composed in the bitterness of mourning Percy, who had drowned at sea. As she ponders her own, unbearable isolation Mary turns to a vivid, even brutal dissection of what it might mean to be the sole survivor of a world laid waste. 'My thoughts are a sealed treasure, which I can confide to none' she wrote on October 2, 1822, the first journal entry she was to make after 'the fatal 8th'. She considers the expressive power of language, 'dark imagery' with which she must 'blot' the whiteness of the page. She is unsure about her powers: 'But can I express all I feel?' (*MSJ*.180,181)

The depression that weighed her down in the years following Shelley's death, must have stemmed in part from feeling that she bore within her a whole life that had vanished from plain sight. Elsewhere in the journal she writes of how her clear image of Shelley 'mocks reality'. (*MSJ*.184) Death, to which she was no stranger, forged an 'internal life', more vivid and vital than her emotionally impoverished existence. (*MSJ*.183)

The sight of old friends could only serve to remind her of her abrupt, brutal loss: 'Seeing Coleridge last night reminded me forcibly of past times', she notes in a journal entry for January 18, 1824. She mourns a lost self, her genius driven underground: 'My imagination is dead, my genius lost, my energies sleep'. (*MSJ*.192) The English landscape is cold, constricting, lacking in the sublimity that Italy ('dear Italy, murderess of those I love') granted her. There in spite of memories of loss in the contemplation of beauty, pain lost its corrosive edge and imagination flourished:

> Then I could think, and my imagination could invent and combine, and self became absorbed in the grandeur of the universe I created. Now, my mind is a blank, a gulf filled with formless mist.
> The last man! Yes, I may well describe that solitary being's feelings, feeling myself as the last relic of a beloved race, my companions extinct before me. (*MSJ*.193)

Her use of the term 'imagination' draws on Coleridge's celebrated formulation in the *Biographia Literaria* (1817) but by reversing its implications. Where Coleridge had written of the secondary imagination as summoning up the primary perceptual materials of the world ('it dissolves, diffuses, dissipates in order to recreate') Mary Shelley stresses the mind's own stuff, its inventions, placing the verb 'invent' first, following it up with the verb 'combine'. (*BL*.304) The natural world offers a spur, but nothing of substance to the imagination's labour. The absorption of self is in 'the grandeur of the universe I created.'

Yet it would be a mistake to see Mary Shelley's notion of 'imagination' as a clear development of the Wordsworthian 'egotistical sublime'. Far from being 'a thing per se that stands alone' Mary Shelley's consciousness, like that of her mother and of Dorothy Wordsworth, exhibits the relational bonds that characterise a feminine imagination. Grown feverish here, through loss and isolation, it is nevertheless present, if only as a negativity to a blank existence, a 'gulf filled with formless mist'. It is within this context that she develops her vision of Perdita as an embodiment of femininity. Torn by her inability to express what was within her, Perdita watches as human love and civilised order slowly crumble in the wake of plague and 'promiscuous death'.

Early in *The Last Man*, Mary Shelley, with her fondness for the embedded quotation, evokes the power if not the precise sentiments of a precursor by citing the middle stanza of Wordsworth's 'She dwelt among the untrodden ways'. Though she acknowledges the iconic power of Wordsworth's image, she questions what she sees as the implied unity of the modest, half hidden violet and the exposed beauty of the single star in the night sky. For the poet, each image exhibits a different facet of the vanished beloved. For Lionel Verney, the narrator of the novel, the discrepant nature of the images seems noteworthy: 'Wordsworth has compared a beloved female to two fair objects in nature; but his lines always appeared to me rather a contrast than a similitude'. (*LM*.36)

Perdita who represents the complicated, introverted nature of femininity, is likened to a modest violet. Quite distinct is Idris, continually idealised in the novel by the adoring Lionel, her magnificence most like Wordsworth's solitary star. Though the contrasting modes are not always worked out consistently, each character represents a different strategy by which women may seek knowledge in the world.

While Idris by and large is what she seems, Perdita covers over her true self in characteristically feminine posture. The terrible intensity of her emotions finds no outlet in the world. Perdita's sexual passion for Raymond, who is obsessed by power and the claims of territoriality, makes her lose herself in his being. Such severe absorption of the feminine self entails the destructuring of the autonomous self and the invasive reality of another who holds dominion. It was a condition which Mary Shelley was intimately aware of.

In her attempt to mark out the sexual tension that femininity was heir to, Mary Shelley highlights the boundaries between public and private realms in bold, even simplistic fashion. Raymond, terrified by what he cannot control, tries to kill love for the sake of ambition: 'Love! I must steel my heart against *that* . . . that is to say the love which would rule me, not that which I rule.' (*LM*.39) His initial resolve is to marry Idris, whose royal blood could further his political aims. But as his passion for Perdita grows, he is thrown into severe self-doubt, 'slave' as he puts it to 'this over-ruling heart'. His voice, his body entire, reveal 'a strong, internal conflict'. (*LM*.45) For her part, Perdita demands that he choose between her and his worldly ambitions. As their love grows, she remakes her self in the 'still pool' of Raymond's eyes, 'drinking in with rapture the reflection there made of the form of herself and her lover, shewn for the first time in dear conjunction.' (*LM*.48)

When their daughter Clara is born, one of the strongest impulses of her maternity is to recover Raymond's features in their daughter. At birth Clara was 'an embryo copy', the narrator tells us, of her father. Yet this imprinting of female flesh with the male image, this recasting of the feminine self in the male gaze, exacts its own cost. As the precarious balance of her domestic life is ruptured, with Raymond's attentions more and more absorbed by the public world where he now holds sway as the Lord Protector of England, Perdita finds it hard to reconcile what she is to herself with what she might be in the world: 'Her internal pride and humility of manner were now more than ever at war.' (*LM*.75)

The imbalance between what is hidden within and what is exhibited to the world, even as it marks out a feminine trauma reveals the Romantic roots of Perdita's characterisation. While the male poets worked out elaborate, at times conflicting myths of inwardness and the outer world, the imagination and the external forces it had to contend with, they were never faced with the female problem of representing both the tension of a dialectical creativity and the perils of a consciousness that had to grasp itself as secondary, even subservient, in a gendered world.

*   *   *

There is an important woman character in *The Last Man*, to be set against Perdita's femininity. It is Evadne, the young Greek woman of patrician descent, who falls in love with Raymond. Bit by bit she draws Raymond away from Perdita, her passion pulling him away from his former self. Almost without conscious knowledge, Raymond responds to her need. 'The territory of his own heart', the narrator tells us, 'escaped his notice'. (*LM*.84)

The web of deceit he spins to hide his involvement from Perdita, finally destroys his own self-integrity. But though his passionate self undermines him and his deceit is gradually revealed Raymond sustains his masculine dominance in Perdita's eyes. She cannot be without him, she cries, simply at the mercy of 'my own wretched engrossing self'. (*LM*.102)

To gain Raymond's notice Evadne, a self-taught artist, now living in abject poverty, sends him architectural plans for the grand museum of the arts he hopes to construct. The plans are sent under anonymous cover. But something in the drawing moves Raymond. He seeks out the artist and discovers the Evadne he once knew, noble still, engrossed in her art, but living in a bare, tattered room.

Years later this independent artistic woman dies in delirium on the battlefields of Constantinople, her body disguised in a male warrior's clothing. Her artistic talents unfulfilled, haunted by passion, she has followed Raymond on to the battle field. Lionel, viewing the devastation caused by man, 'the corse-strewn earth . . . felt ashamed of my species.' The glorious calm of nature seems to castigate human folly. He hears a terrible shriek, 'a form seemed to rise from the earth'. Lionel discovers the lost, dying

Evadne. In her delirium, hearing English speech, she thinks it Raymond. She cries out to him: 'Many living deaths have I borne for thee, O Raymond, and now I expire, thy victim! – By my death I purchase thee – lo! the instruments of war, fire, the plague are my servitors . . . ' (LM.131)

In a passion that can never be redeemed, the woman artist dies, invoking cosmic powers of destruction. Her suffering and death must purchase her lover. The governing strategy of *The Last Man* makes use of a similar equation. Death can right the balance of unredeemable loss, restore in another kingdom what has been taken away so cruelly from this one. And art must kindle and burnish what is left of the pitiful human soul.

Close to the end of the novel as the survivors struggle up the mountainside they come upon a small chapel. Strains of Hayden's 'New-Created World' flow from it. A young woman, on the brink of death is playing to her blind old father, described as a man 'whose soul was ear'. (LM.306) The strains of Romantic creation can scarcely mask in sublime forgetfulness the end that must surely occur.

If as Burke suggested the consciousness of death under-writes all experiences of the sublime, then sublimity is given, for a brief space, to the woman musician. Yet she creates in a condition of anguish, her body already diseased, its corrupting physicality unappeasable. Self-consciousness cannot redeem her. She too is subject to the central, invasive symbol of the novel, a relentless plague that can only be brought to an end when humankind itself is vanquished.

Mary Shelley's *Mathilda*

Is there a female Oedipus? Mary Shelley would have answered in the affirmative. *Mathilda* (1819), a novella that Godwin effectively suppressed because he was disturbed by its overt depiction of father–daughter incest, begins with a heroine who identifies herself with Oedipus: 'Oedipus [the speaker herself] is about to die'.

But the narrator, Mathilda is also a fresh incarnation of Wordsworth's Lucy: 'I live in a lone cottage on a solitary, wide heath: no voice of life reaches me.'[6] Indeed no less than three of the 'Lucy' poems, each with its version of the iconic feminine, are invoked in the course of this deadly autobiography. The fusion of the Romantic feminine with prohibited passion, father–daughter incest in particular, was fresh in Mary Shelley's mind. She started composing *Mathilda* in August, 1819, the very month in which Percy completed his poetic drama *The Cenci*, in which Beatrice, raped by her father, exacts vengeance and is herself condemned to death. 'My father's spirit/His eye, his voice, his touch surrounding me;/The atmosphere and breath of my dead life!' Beatrice cries out on hearing of the Pope's command that she must die. Unnatural patriarchal power condemns the tender young Beatrice to death. To Shelley the cruelty of passion seems to fulfil 'the highest moral purpose' that drama can aim at: 'teaching the human heart, through its sympathies and antipathies, the knowledge of itself.' (*S*.298,240)

But while Beatrice feels real hatred for a father whose lust is motivated by the desire for dominance, Mathilda feels intense longing for her father. The novella in which the heroine acts out her passion and impending death, draws its morbid power from the way in which the presences of father and mother, the one sexually dominant, tormented, and utterly alive even when far away, the other dead, but invasive in her absence, conjointly destroy the narrator.

Mathilda is a feminine myth of origin, but one in which the quest for self leads to a past that can only evict the fragile subjectivity from whatever small space it has for itself. Her involvement in her father's passion for her, and the 'crime [of] . . . involuntary feeling' promise to reveal her origin. (*M*.25) Mathilda's mother Diana died in childbirth, and the father totally identifies the daughter with his dead beloved. But Mathilda can no more fuse with Diana, however inflamed a father's passion, than Mary Shelley can become her own mother. This desire becomes its own death, the 'chasm' into which Mathilda's father falls, permitting a final, inevitable recognition:

> In my madness I dared to say to myself – Diana died to give her birth; her mother's spirit was transferred into her frame, and she ought to be as Diana to me. With every effort to cast it off, this love clings closer, this guilty love more unnatural than hate, that withers your hopes and destroys me forever . . . oh, thou soul of my soul: thou in whom I breathe! (*M*.40-1)

By voicing his desire, Mathilda's father reveals the fragile boundaries of flesh, spells out an exacting economy that even as it fulfils the daughter's unspeakable longing, must destroy her. As a young child Mathilda was cast into the care of a harsh aunt: 'to a timid child she was as a plant beneath a thick covering of ice; I should cut my hands in endeavouring to get at it.' (*M*.9) The young girl, if less bookish than Wollstonecraft's Mary, survives like her fictive predecessor by discovering a harbour in nature: 'I bore an individual attachment to every tree in our park; every animal that inhabited it knew me and I loved them.' Then follows an overt allusion to a 'Lucy' poem with an authorial footnote that clearly identifies the poetic source: 'I lived', Mathilda, explains to her readers 'in a desolate country where there were none to praise/And very few to love.' (*M*.9)

In gaining sustenance from nature, Mathilda is able to compensate for her unnatural fate. Maternal nature can repair human wounds. Modest, reticent like Lucy, she is a dreamy child, given to long fantasies about her absent parents. Knowing she can never again see her mother, she lingers on the thought of her absent father, 'the idol of my imagination'. (*M*.11) She dreams of dressing like a boy and wandering through the world in search of him. Over and over she images the moving scene of recognition. The instrument of recognition, a miniature she wears exposed on her breast, bears pondering.

In *Frankenstein* the monster just after he has murderd little William, discovers a locket, a miniature of a lovely woman around the dead boy's neck: it bears the image of his beautiful dead mother. Recognition of the child's human origin, further arouses the monster's rage. He senses his own irreversible alienation. His form he knows is nothing more or less than a 'filthy type' of his creator's.

In the Godwin household, the portrait of the dead Mary Wollstonecraft was placed prominently on the mantelpiece. Day in, day out, the growing Mary confronted the lovely image of her mother. Her own face pale, more delicate, less extravagant in its sensuality, must have served her as a palimpsest. There were surely moments when Mary sought her mother in herself, using the stern Godwin to whom she was passionately attached as a kind of bridge. There are indications in her life and letters of the great pleasure she took in any recognition that she was like her mother. In August 1823 she writes to Leigh Hunt of her delight at the remarks of Louisa, wife of the playwright James Kenney: 'Mrs K. says that I am grown very like my Mother, especially in Manners – in my way of addressing people – this is the most flattering thing anyone could say to me.'[7]

To satisfy the father's desire might be to truly replace the mother, repair the terrible damage that the very act of coming to life had caused: 'Until I met Shelley I may justly say that he was my God – and I remember many childish instances of the excess of attachment I bore for him', Mary wrote of Godwin, to her friend Jane Williams. From time to time she was keenly aware of the 'excessive and romantic attachment' she had felt for her father. (*MSL*.1:296,2:215)

If her father's image, worn on her breast, serves as a visible and outward mark of who she is and to whom she belongs, that talisman is transformed into a cruel brand after Mathilda's recognition of her father's sexual passion for her. The irony is that the mark is invisible to all but Mathilda herself. Passive to a fault, obedient to her father's authority, she seems to herself to suffer a dreadful fall through no fault of her own: 'I disobeyed no command, I ate no apple, and yet I was ruthlessly driven from it [Paradise].' (*M*.16) She is marked then for life, as Cain was: 'like another Cain, I had a mark set on my forehead'. (*M*.71) She becomes a pariah, an outcast from the shared world, turned grotesque in recognition of her father's desire: 'Monster as I am, you are still, as you ever were, lovely, beautiful beyond expression' her father had whispered to her as he fainted away. (*M*.31) But Mathilda knows better: she has changed beyond any self she could have wanted.

Or has she? Is it possible that what she perceives as moral deformity is really a secret source of power? Her existence turned to a fatal secret, Mathilda becomes skilled at the craft of subterfuge. Feminine to the core, or so it seems to those who look on her, she locks within her heart knowledge of a passion that no woman within the charmed circle of femininity should hold. Raped in mind, if not body, by her father's desire, she stands as an emblem of the eternal feminine.

Implicit knowledge of her condition, even as it cuts her off forever from the shared world, grants an indissoluble power over her own being. Once 'Nursling of Nature's bright self' Mathilda like a surreal version of Dr Gregory's model woman, must try to cover up her secret life with 'an impenetrable heap of false smiles and words: cunning frauds, treacherous laughter and a mixture

of all light deceits . . a mist to blind others'. (*M*.47) As
Victor protected his monster, so Mathilda must cover up
a monstrous knowledge of desire: 'I with my dove's look
and fox's heart.' (*M*.48)

She dresses in nun's clothing and gradually finds
herself drawn to a suffering young poet of elevated
sentiments. But if Woodville is a thinly veiled depiction
of Shelley, Mathilda/Mary skilled at the arts of subterfuge
sees through Woodville's longing, his desire to pose her in
a setting of his own fabrication, to frame her:

> I am, I thought, a tragedy; a character that he comes
> to see act: now and then he gives me my cue that I
> may make a speech more to his purpose: perhaps he
> is already planning a poem in which I am to figure. I
> am a farce and play to him, but to me this is all dreary
> reality: he takes all the profit and I bear all the burthen
> (*M*.65)

After such knowledge, what forgiveness? The gentleness
and goodness Mathilda acknowledges in Woodville, cannot
compete with the heroine's own absorption in herself. She
sets the scene for her own purposes. She compares herself to
Persephone who was 'gaily gathering flowers . . . when the
King of Hell snatched her.' (*M*.31) But while Persephone
was mourned for by her mother, ransomed by that Goddess
from the halls of Hell, Mathilda finds herself utterly alone.
The myth rewritten has brought no comfort. Fusion with
the dead mother cannot rebeget the self. Yet the cycles of
repetition are fierce and unrelenting in this female fable.
The father whose return had granted her an entirely new
dispensation of life, a new birth even it had seemed ('I felt
as if I were recreated and had about me all the freshness and
life of a new being') returns her to her mother's house, 'the
rooms which my mother had inhabited'. (*M*.16,23)

The house/body trope is not irrelevant here. Mathilda in

her emptiness finds her own body filling out with passion as she follows her father's desire. And her father, speaking to her much as Wordsworth's Plutonic Nature might have done in 'Three Years She Grew . . . ', plays out his own version of nature's desire: 'you seemed to have gained a grace from the mountain breezes – the waterfalls and the lake.' (*M*.38)

Lest we lose the echo, a third 'Lucy' poem enters the text, this time as direct quotation. Preparing herself for death, the price of her passionate trespass, Mathilda takes comfort in the fact that she will be carried back into the womb of nature: 'Rolled round in earth's diurnal course . . . ' The quotation from Wordsworth's 'A Slumber did My Spirit Seal' is explicit. Mathilda lovingly evokes the maternal earth. Her 'emaciated body' can rest in death on earth's 'bosom': 'For it will be the same with thee, who art called our Universal Mother, when I am gone. I have loved thee . . . and all my dreams which have often strangely deformed thee, will die with me'. (*M*.76-7) Safe in the arms of nature, Mathilda can give up the burden of her individual consciousness, her tormented sexuality, the deformity forced on her by the acceptance of a patriarchal protection. It is noteworthy though, that such entry into nature requires a renunciation of motion and force.

Through the subterfuge of femininity, through the wily use of appearances, Mathilda finally prepares to enter her mother's home. It is her tragedy, however, that such entry cannot be granted to her lively, separate self. Flattened out, evicted from her bodily hold on the world, Mathilda ekes out her days, like Lucy, on a lonely heath. But it is Lucy revised, for under the feminine modesty, under the silence and calm, lies the unappeasable turbulence of Wollonstonecraft's daughter.

8 Versions of the Sublime

'Something Getting Free'

In the quest for the sublime women writers were curiously recalcitrant. By and large they withdrew from a vision that seemed to reach, without mediation to divinity. The grand marriages of sense and spirit, 'a culminating and procreative marriage between mind and nature', as M.H. Abrams calls it, are typically absent in female writing.[1] Rather, there is a crossing back, at the brink of visionary revelation, to the realms of ordinary, bodily experience – whether that experience is rendered subtle and elusive, as with Dorothy Wordsworth, or imaged in almost brutal excess, as with Mary Shelley. Typically then, such writing chooses to preserve rather than forget the materials of ordinary female life. And this choice, implicit, even covert at times, restructures a new feminine sensibility. When women do write of sublimity, there is frequently apprehension, a tightening of tone as if permission were sought from a patriarchal power.

Thomas Weiskel has argued for an understanding of the Romantic sublime as 'a major analogy, a massive transposition of transcendence into a naturalistic key.' He goes on to point out that 'the affective aggrandisement of the sublime moment supports an illusion, a metaphorical union with the creator which suppresses the inferiority of our status as listeners.'[2] This simultaneous loss of self and fusion with a transcendent power is sustained by a void in the soul that characterises the Romantic sublime. It is typically seen in the reflexive preoccupations of Wordsworth or Shelley, who in their differing ways absolve themselves of all that stands outside consciousness, tugging at it, limiting its free scope. The only pressures admitted within the charmed circle of meaning-making are the internal rhythms of thought and desire. These rhythms, as the poets were astute enough to realise, gained authenticity to the extent to which they scrupulously adhered to an ever changing perception of reality. And part of that reality was undoubtedly the world of others.

In *Letters on the Improvement of the Mind* (1773) Hester Chapone suggests that a young woman who seeks to educate herself properly should be open to the contemplation of the natural world. Mere propriety was not good enough for the growing consciousness of the young girl; the religious sensibility had to be stirred. Chapone remarks on the 'most sublime entertainment' thhat may be had in gazing at the delights of nature, its arrangements so acute that art could never hope to mimic the wonders of the simplest leaf visible to the eye. Lest it be thought that Hester Chapone's enthusiasm for the natural world, for what Sampson Reed was to call its 'cabinet of creation' was purely transcendentalist in nature, I should hasten to add that the hidden agenda in her work was the 'Almighty Hand' of God the Father.[3]

Yet such an emphasis cannot diminish the very real 'astonishment and rapture' she claims she has gained from her 'experiment' in raising her eyes to the heavens. The sudden glimpse of cosmic order has filled her with feelings she cannot set to words: 'It is impossible to describe the sensation I felt from the glorious, boundless prospect of infinite beneficence bursting at once upon my imagination!' But the voice continues, drawing back sharply from the loss of hierarchy, the vacancy of a boundless universe, the terror even that such sublimity must entail. She turns instead to the anthropomorphic divinity ('that great and good Being') who exerts a firm and comforting authority. Patriarchal permission is implicitly sought for the shock of feeling.[4]

Well before the composition of her earliest works, Mary Wollstonecraft had read and admired writers like Hester Chapone, Sarah Trimmer and Mrs Barbauld, who espoused a belief that women could exalt their spirit through openness to a religious sublimity, through awe at the boundless powers of the deity. In *Mary, A Fiction* the young heroine witnesses the terrible storm and the ensuing destruction. She feels the precariousness of her own life: 'Eternity, immateriality, and happiness – what are ye?' she ponders in one of her fragments of writing. 'How shall I grasp the mighty and fleeting conceptions ye create?' The outburst relaxes her and she is able to sleep, her soul 'delivered . . . into the hands of the Father of Spirits'. (*MWW*.47)

While this first novel exhibits Wollstonecraft's characteristic self-division, the conflict between her need to express the truth of the heart and internalised edicts of patriarchy that would at best assuage, at worst suppress that truth, it would be wrong I think, to assume that her experience of the sublime was inhibited solely by such authority. In *Letters from Sweden* we see how the feminine consciousness reaches out for rich, humane reasons for withdrawing from the Romantic sublime. The appropriation of divinity would cut her loose from the substantial, relational world of loved others, a realm of concrete nurture and care. Most often these others are female, near at hand or imagined, their existences stitching the speaker back into a shared world of troubled experience. The infant Fanny's femaleness was a special cause for concern. 'I dread to unfold her mind', Wollstonecraft confesses, a mother's qualms about the fate of a young daughter bubbling to the surface. Nurturing her to the innocence that the contemplation of beauty can bestow might be to render her 'unfit for the world she is to inhabit – Hapless woman!' (L.55) Even sublimity and the power it brings might hurt given 'the oppressed state of my sex' (L.160) Yet these reflections were etched against the backdrop of a landscape overtly grasped as maternal, a nature that disclosed itself as the 'nurse of sentiment'. (L.58) Wollstonecraft is fascinated by the possible beginning of things. She reflects on the 'active principle' that keeps her awake though all of nature is at rest. (L.16) Her spirit is so restless, so vibrant that she cannot conceive of annihilation. She ponders the terror of death:

> I cannot bear to think of being no more – of losing myself – though existence is often but a painful consciousness of misery; nay it appears to me impossible that I should cease to exist . . . (L.76)

The longing to believe quickens her gaze, a delicate detail of jellyfish below the water's surface as she rows her boat. The creatures seem almost 'thickened water'. She notices the whitish edge to them, framing 'four purple circles, of different forms . . . over an incredible number of fibres or white lines.' Their vivid texture in water fades when she lifts them out with a ladle. They dwindle into 'colourless jelly'. (L.76)

Quite early in her travels she remarks on the primordial character of the landscape. The ocean and the dark rocks seem 'rude materials of creation forming the barrier of unwrought space'. (L.10) A later encounter suggests the dawn of creation, the 'first efforts of sportive nature'. (L.40) The closer she gets to the ocean the more the earth strips itself. To approach the origin is to close in on death.

Now the relational character of the authorial consciousness is clarified. Her genius is not isolate. It is gripped by loved others, even those beyond the grave. Imagination becomes a necessity, reworking the awesome emotion of loss into a landscape which both evokes and sustains it. The two Fannys, the friend long dead and the infant named for her (parted now from her mother in the exigencies of rough overland travel) meet in Wollstonecraft's consciousness as pain is wrought into inscription:

> The grave has closed over a dear friend, the friend of my youth; still she is present with me, and I hear her soft voice warbling as I stray over the heath. Fate has separated me from another, the fire of whose eyes, tempered by infantine tenderness, still warms my breast; even when gazing on those tremendous cliffs, sublime emotions absorb my soul. (*L*.59)

The theme of death stitches through *Letters*. 'So short a residence', the author noted in the Advertisement to the work, its brevity indicative of the span of life itself. The 'I' stands out in relief against a mortality which both annihilates and sets free. A 'something getting free', she calls it quite simply in the fifteenth letter, life being an imprisonment that a finer, annihilating element will not tolerate. Wollstonecraft notes the fine white lines of the aging pines, their 'cobweb-like appearance', the saplings struggling for existence, huge masses of torn stones sheltering them, portions of a cyclic life her very being shares in. Hence the reflection on death etching in the freedom she longs for:

> I cannot tell why, – but death, under every form, appears to me like some thing getting free . . . I feel that this conscious being must be as unfettered, have the wings of thought before it can be happy. (*L*.132)

The longing to imbue her words with 'the wings of thought' fed into her epistolary style, its associative form perfectly suited to the explorative forays of a

consciousness determined to search out its own version
of truth. Grasping her life in what she thought of as
the middle of her existence, Wollstonecraft sets out the
'history of my own heart.' (*L*.90-1) Unlike Wordsworth's
Prelude where the poet speaks of 'the river of my mind'
(*Prel*.11.214), its genesis and ending rounded in the majesty
of verse, Wollstonecraft's *Letters* move in a series of quick,
restless questionings, the centre of selfhood dissolving into
the probings of her voice: 'But whither am I wandering?'
(*L*.55)

The baggage of selfhood that Wordsworth could carry
with him and set down at will to furnish any wilderness of
the mind, is a far cry from what the woman writer needed
for the completion of her knowledge. Indeed the meditative
clarity of *Letters*, the attentive vision, the refusal to project
the self outwards into the encircling landscapes, all point
forward to Dorothy's journals. There is a further link,
the compassionate, brief but recurrent glimpses of human
others. In the *Grasmere Journals*, Dorothy frequently uses
her passing observation of a woman or young child, or even
the words of a traveller, to tell of human pain or deprivation.
As she journeys with William towards France and Annette,
she notes the words of a fellow traveller: 'A woman on the
top of the coach said to me: "It is a sad thing for the
poor people for the hop-gathering is the women's harvest,
there is employment about the hops both for women and
children." ' (*AGJ*.151)

In *Letters* Wollstonecraft's glimpses of the women she
meets in passing or even just imagines in her wanderings,
are precise and compassionate, cut free of the rhetoric
of *Vindication*. As with Dorothy, female labour becomes
emblematic of natural difficulty. Wollstonecraft considers
the chapped hands of Swedish women who must wash
linen in the ice-cold river water, an imagined detail but
one that gathers a rich emotive power to it – stopped
short though of the convolutions of full-blown symbolism.

Elsewhere Wollstonecraft notices a young mother in the inn at Tonsberg. Forced to work as a wet nurse to earn her keep, she farms out her own baby. The child's father has abandoned them. Trapped in 'this most painful state of widowhood', she cuts a poignant figure. The author hears her hum a 'melancholy ditty'. Glimpsing her own self in this female other Wollstonecraft writes of hastening outdoors, unable to bear the pressure of emotion. She must take her 'solitary evening's walk'. (L.80)

The choice of phrase is not accidental. Mary Wollstonecraft was well acquainted with Rousseau's *Reveries of the Solitary Walker* (1782), and behind the rambling heroine of *Letters* stands Rousseau's *promeneur solitaire*. In his Second Walk Rousseau tells of keeping a record of his lonely rambles and of inscribing the reveries that fill him when his head is left 'entirely free and . . . my ideas follow their bent without resistance or constraint'.[5] His method was to find a powerful echo in Wollstonecraft's vision of the unfettered 'flow' of thoughts. Yet happiness for Rousseau – a man cut from a shared life, deliberately exiled – came from a solipsistic feeding 'on my own substance'. (*SW*.111) For Wollstonecraft, in contrast, moments of bliss when the soul sensed its perfect equipoise, could only be supported within the mesh of relational being. In Rousseau's strain she describes a solitude in which 'the imagination bodies forth its conceptions unrestrained, and stops enraptured to adore the beings of its own creation.' (*L*.85) But while these were 'moments of bliss', she was acutely conscious that such ecstasy was flickering, and even held danger. There is a 'misery, as well as rapture', she writes, to be glimpsed in the sublime.

The tension between Romantic insight and a hard won realism remains in Wollstonecraft's thought. Yet to walk abroad like Rousseau's solitary was an important freedom for the writing woman, one that underwrote her capacity to create. Indeed, as for Dorothy Wordsworth, the ordinary, earthly freedom to walk, was most precious to the feminine imagination. An unearthly sublimity, transfixed by divine sanctions, seemed far less enticing.

The phrase 'Solitary Walker' is evoked again by Mary Wollstonecraft, a year later in August 1796. In the crush of her beginning attachment to Godwin, fearful lest the strength of passion which had turned physical, destroy his respect for her, she writes that he'd best forget her. If only he could write off what occurred as one of the 'slight mortal shakes to which you are liable', she herself could put on the garb of a 'Solitary Walker' once again. (*WL*.337) The phrase is underlined in the letter, its sense quite clear to both writer and intimate reader. The figure of walking out and at will, best expressed for Wollstonecraft the restless spirit that animated her life and thought.

'More than Natural Loveliness' (Dorothy Wordsworth)

In her *Alfoxden Journal*, in an entry for February 26, 1798, Dorothy Wordsworth speaks of a clear afternoon when she walks with Coleridge almost all the way to Stowey. She tells of lying 'sidelong on the turf', unable to gaze at 'the landscape till it melted into more than natural loveliness.' In the picturesque tradition she was well versed in, she describes the precise tint of the ocean, 'a pale greyish blue, the single bay, bright and blue like the sky' regretting only the lack of a sailing ship, 'a perfect image of delight' to complete the picture. The companions stroll to the height of a hill to view a fortification, then sit down, utterly freed of other claims on their time to 'feed on the prospect'. (*AGJ*.8)

Dorothy's phrase prefigures William's lines in 'Tintern Abbey'. Returning to the Wye valley the poet ponders a moment from which he may gather 'life and food/For

future years'. But while the poetic voice muses on the
'picture of the mind', that perplexing, even potentially
hazardous process by which consciousness discovers meaning within itself, recognising finally a sublimity that might
validate consciousness, Dorothy keeps quite chastely to
the givenness of things, drawing back from speculation.
(*PW*.2:261) Indeed her mind recoils, almost fearful in
spite of the companionable presence of Coleridge, that
most abstruse of Romantic thinkers. Once again, the
integrity of her vision sustains a resolutely private tone.
Consciousness, even as it is drawn forward fascinated,
relinquishes a further quest. Dorothy describes what lies
before her: 'a magnificent scene curiously spread out for
even minute inspection, though so extensive that the mind
is afraid to calculate its bounds.' (*AGJ*.8)

Elsewhere in the *Alfoxden Journal*, again walking with
Coleridge, she tells of a 'mild morning'. From a hill top
she observes the sea. At first shrouded in mist, it gradually
appears to her, shot free of the vapour. The flickering
elements of earth, sky and sea slip in and out of visibility.
The land that is cleared stands in as a darker simulacrum
of cloud, underwriting the motion of actual clouds. 'I never
saw such a union of earth, sky and sea', writes Dorothy:
'The clouds beneath our feet spread themselves to the water
and the clouds of the sky almost joined them.' (*AGJ*.4-5)
The writer's perspective is implied quite precisely as she
celebrates the almost mystical blending of the elements –
she stands on a hill, higher than the lowest clouds, the
ocean dropping away under foot. Conventional expectations
of gender dissolve. Coleridge the male companion is utterly
silent. The silence extends to the perceived landscape.

It is as if her 'I' drew vitality from an emptying
out of itself, a total abnegation of the all too human
need to measure and control. Now value shines forth.
The line 'Gathered sticks in the wood; a perfect stillness'
follows on. The simple task of picking up sticks for the

household fires gathers grace and luminosity, occurring as it does after the glimpse of the unity of the elements. The 'perfect stillness' the writer notes comes not just from an absence of noise but from a supernal peace that the woman has just witnessed and borne away within her self. Boundaries between inner and outer realms are dissolved as the household task of gathering sticks is accomplished out of doors, sanctified by being set within the locus of vision.

There are numerous examples in Dorothy's journals of simple acts of perception raised to an almost visionary level. In these passages subjectivity is cast into an *époche*, a phenomenological bracket, so that self rather than the world, is suspended.[6] Yet rather than a lack, or an erasure, this betokens a finely wrought strategy, almost a spiritual task.

In her book *Waiting for God*, Simone Weil, the French mystic and religious thinker, formulated a privileged quality of attention in which 'the soul empties itself of all of its own contents in order to receive into itself the being it is looking at'. This act of decreation involves a withdrawal of the human will, renouncing a posture we find hard to do without, 'our imaginary position as centre'. A change in perception occurs when the will is given up and the self is able to renounce its imagined centrality:

A transformation then takes place at the very roots of our sensibility, in our immediate reception of sense impressions and psychological impressions. It is a transformation analogous to that which takes place in the dusk of evening on a road, where we suddenly discern as a tree what we had at first seen as a stooping man; or where we suddenly recognise as a rustling of leaves what we thought at first was whispering voices. We see the same colours; we hear the same sounds, but not in the same way.[7]

Giving up an anthropocentric hold on the world is crucial to the revelation of being that Simone Weil sought. At privileged moments in Dorothy Wordsworth's journal, it is precisely this same mode that seems to function, gathering power from her lucid descriptions. The poverty of human knowledge frees the mind to trust its own finitude, and the visible world is crystallised into a series of sharp, faceted fragments. In the entries that compose the *Alfoxden and Grasmere Journals*, the very structure of the journal form – impressions or episodes strung on the line of a continuous outer chronology, without any overt dependence on memory – permits, even invites the sharp broken fragments that tell of the perceived landscape, elliptical displacements through which the writer, with her compelling reticence unfolds on to the visible world minute discriminations that hint at the mind's meaning-making power. Fragments become her vehicle for intensity, though at times their cryptic nature can make them difficult to decipher.

In the course of a sustained reflection on the fragment and its status in Romanticism, Thomas McFarland points out how 'the logic of incompleteness is . . . ultimately the logic of infinity'.[8] But if in the poetry of Wordsworth and Coleridge the infinity that is evoked lies beyond a visionary border, ingathered though through the compulsions of imaginative knowledge, in Dorothy Wordsworth's work the procedure seems reversed. Keeping her hold on the actual, given world of perception, she raises the practicalities of a woman's life, the details of domesticity and household labour out of their sunken invisibility, into a finer knowledge. She does not divide the inner and outer worlds. Indeed the form of the journal where ordinary perceptions are strung along an implicit thread of outer chronology, without any pressure to raise them to a symbolic level, was helpful in preserving the bounds of her perceptual world. The claims of privacy could be respected without any burdensome dragging after meaning.

The haunting scene she witnesses at the funeral of an anonymous woman opens with a detail drawn from the world of practical female duties. The writer has been ironing clothes: 'I ironed until 1/2 past three – now very hot.' As she moves to the scene of the funeral in a poor person's house, the pressure of emotion works into the rhythm of observation. There are details about guests, the plain food that is served, the black painted coffin covered with a cloth. Now the observer is drawn in, more deeply than is ordinarily her fashion, death drawing her on to contemplate the final isolation of a human life: 'I was affected to tears . . . There were no near kindred, no children.' But the dark interior is left behind as the coffin is borne outdoors and the sunlight turns the landscape, 'more sacred than I had ever seen it, and yet more allied to human life'.

This complex perception arising out of an acute sense of mortality as it cuts against the persistence of the natural world, is simply left there, as for the first time sorrow is released in tears, the femaleness of the dead person acknowledged, another woman, kindred to the self, anonymous, perishing into earth: 'I thought she was going to a quiet spot and could not help weeping very much.' (*AGJ*.38) But the voice moves on, noting the progress of the funeral party, the unkempt mien of the parson drunk in the pub just the day before. Then the whole is edged by a domestic notation, repeating the task of the day that the writer has left behind her. She must return to the home, to the task of ironing which continues till late into the evening: 'I had not finished ironing till 7 o'clock.' (*AGJ*.39)

Visiting La Mer de Glace (the Shelleys)

The Romantic poets discovered within the recesses of subjectivity notions of privacy and passion that bound them to creative power, at least in terms of the mythology they established. If the world was hostile, inwardness, at least moment by moment, could recast perception and memory in a myth of meaning-making, whether it was the natural piety that William Wordsworth sometimes had recourse to, or the negativities of symbol that Percy Shelley discovered for himself. In 'Mont Blanc, Lines Written in the Vale of Chamonix' a poem composed in Switzerland in July 1816, Shelley meditates on how the meaning of poetry works its way into consciousness. The extremities of Alpine landscape permit him the intense symbolic alterations of meaning, the flux of emotion, the scepticism that still believes in a fiction of the mind's own making. While there are allusions to Wordsworth's 'Tintern Abbey' clear discrepancies exist between these two great poetic meditations of English Romanticism. In Wordsworth's poem the 'picture of the mind' with its glimpses of meaning-making emerges within the shelter of a given place ('while here I stand'). For Shelley there is effectively no place to stand. Beneath – if the voice without detriment to the fierce symbolic internalisations can be considered as issuing from a particular place – lies the ravine of Arve, filled with restless, 'ceaseless motion'. Above, looms the icy mountain range, stripped bare of all that might support human life: 'many a precipice,/Frost and the Sun in scorn of mortal power/Have piled: dome, pyramid and pinnacle,/A city of death.' And the disembodied spirit, is 'driven', the verb Shelley uses, back and forth in relentless passage.

The power of the mind, accumulates not in a contemplation that has recourse to a landscape of fierce attachment and unstinting love, as in Wordsworth, but in a vertiginous and desolate fantasy, internal counterpart of a place that offers no habitation: 'Dizzy ravine! and when I gaze on thee/I seem as in a trance sublime and strange/To muse on my own separate fantasy'. (S.90)

Nature itself is scarred and fraught, its primeval substances giving birth to ruin, destruction, and massive irreducible deprivation – at least from the standpoint of human life and all that is needed to spare and preserve it. And the voice is cast back on to a knowledge that is groundless, flickering in a void, able to listen only to the 'mysterious tongue' of the wilderness:

> Which teaches awful doubt, or faith so mild,
> So solemn, so serene, that man may be,
> But for such faith with Nature reconciled. (S.91)

*   *   *

What might it mean to be reconciled with nature? After Wordsworth the question was to haunt others, not just those who lived with him, sharing his daily bread, people like his friend Coleridge or his sister Dorothy, but the second generation of Romantics, as well as the Victorian poets who came after them. Matthew Arnold for instance discovered that the questions put to nature, the pieties drawn from it by Wordsworth, could have no firm basis in his own experience, and was conscious then of an involuntary diminishment where he himself was concerned. A desperate lack, a failing fortitude were what Arnold wrote of, the oceanic ebb of faith lit for a mere instant by sexual love.

Percy Shelley, however, coming soon after Wordsworth, was well sustained by his own invincible sense of poetic genius. Much less susceptible than Arnold to mortal failure, which in any case he could swallow up in the fiery consummations of his poetic vision, Shelley provides images of a natural world which cannot tolerate the consoling pieties Wordsworth had established. His acute glimpse into the 'secret strength of things' permits a ferocity that strips what he sometimes saw as the happy, easeful fictions of a previous generation. The void, the 'vacancy' of a terrible sublime is all too close to him.

In her journal for July 1816, Mary Godwin, not yet married to Percy, records the trip they made to Chamonix and the Mer de Glace. A month earlier she had begun work on her first novel, *Frankenstein, or the Modern Prometheus*. She describes the waters in the ravine of the Arve which 'dashed against its banks like a wild animal who is furious in constraint', the mountains 'higher one would think than the safety of God would permit'. (*MSJ*.51) Two days later on Wednesday, July 24th, they begin the climb to Montanvert. Mary Shelley's sense of natural power, inhospitable, inimical even to human life, both echoes and alters Shelley's own vision. What is important here is a divergence of vision rather than a problem of priority, for as with Dorothy and her brother William, later visitors to the Vale of Chamonix, the questions of shared knowledge and divergent interpretations are both bewildering and illuminating.

Often who said what first, or thought what first, or wrote what first, is far less relevant to the inchoate welter of silence, thought and language in which we all subsist, than sharp meanings drawn from shared experience. Mary notes in her journal how the trees have been ravaged by avalanches: 'some half leaning over others, intermingled with stones, present the appearance of vast and dreadful desolation'. But instead of mining the sight for an expanded sense of desolation, she continues the human line of narrative, following through to the hour when soaked to the skin, she arrives at an inn, and sits down to work on 'my story'. The following day Mary and Percy and '*beaucoup de monde*' continue to Montravert. The weather is far better now, affording a clear view from the summit, a high noon she would not easily forget:

We get to the top at 12, and behold *la Mer de Glace*. This is the most desolate place in the world; iced mountains surround it; no sign of vegetation appears except on the place from which [we] view the scene. We went on the ice; it is traversed by irregular crevices, whose sides of ice appear blue, while the surface is of a dirty white. We dine on the mountain. The air is very cold, yet many flowers grow here, and among others, the rhododendron, or *Rose des Alpes*, in great profusion . . . (*MSJ*.53-4)

Clearly the desolation she witnesses in the Mer de Glace is far from absolute. The sea of ice is framed by the slight vegetation on the mountain where the couple picnic, lightened by splashes of colour from rhododendron petals. The journal consciously maintains the fabric of shared life. It was in her story that the links with a common, ongoing existence, were ruptured.

In precisely the same setting, Victor Frankenstein wanders 'like an evil spirit' haunted by the death of his little brother William. (*F*.90) Like the flesh and blood Shelleys, he too travels towards Montanvert. Nature is magnificent, fit counterpart to his acute and restless sorrow: '*I* was a wreck – but nought had changed in those savage and enduring scenes.' (*F*.4) In a tension that repeats time and again in her work, Mary Shelley writes of a 'maternal nature' that can soothe and comfort in spite of its destructive elements.

Approaching Mont Blanc, Victor recognises an 'awful majesty' in the glittering peaks, the distant icy river. Desolation breeds awe. Awe turns to the sublimity that Burke had written of. But only momentarily. For a human figure intrudes, growing larger and more inimical as it approaches. Then it bursts on to the natural scene splitting open any possible sublime. It is hardly surprising that 'furious detestation and contempt' fill Victor's heart.

Marc Rubenstein has written eloquently of the 'great movement of yearning and searching with respect to motherhood' which he sees as pervading the novel.[9] The *mer de glace* and its homonym *mère* are undoubtedly in

Mary Shelley's mind as on these frozen waters, echoing and amplifying the watery polar wastes that encircle the narrative, Victor comes face to face with the monster he had abandoned at birth.

'I am thy creature . . . Remember, that I am thy creature: I ought to be thy Adam; but I am rather the fallen angel, who thou drivest from joy for no misdeed. Make me happy, and I shall again be virtuous. (*F*.100)

Made from the bits and pieces dredged from charnel houses and animated with the power of scientific will, the creature pleads for a mothering care. The frightened young man, his creator, does not know how to give it.

The 'sublime ecstasy that gave wings to the soul, and allowed it to soar from the obscure world to light and joy' has collapsed into horror, into a peculiarly female vision of the heart of darkness, the utter immersion in substance that gestation, child-bearing and its immediate aftermath involves. (*F*.97) It is a condition consigned to wordlessness, displaced from its centrality in feminine experience and cast on to the margins of culture. The male 'mother' is forced to cower in fear. But, of course, Victor is not a mother nor even a father really, though his ambition was to command the gratitude of a 'new species' as its 'creator and source'. (*F*.54)

★   ★   ★

A little over four years later, Dorothy Wordsworth, who was travelling through Europe with her brother and her sister-in-law, visited the Vale of Chamonix. She too notes the 'beds of the Rosa Alpa, at this season of a very dark green hue with a tinge of brown from the seeds.' Much like the Shelleys, the Wordsworths eat their lunch on the mountain side, actually on the ice now, combining the comforts of food, with a solid approach to natural sublimity. But Romantic domestication of nature is not as safe as it might seem. Dorothy feels her body torn between the extremes of cold – she is seated on the ice – and the heat from the sun. She leaves her companions to sit on a block of granite. When she tries to walk on the waves of ice, the experience is almost vertiginous:

> the view from that distance gives no notion of the height of the waves, or of the depth of the hollows, within which you often look into gulphs of green water, unpiercable, to the bottom, by the sight though translucent as crystal. (*DWJ*.2:286)

The startling danger, the sense of surfaces that conceal impenetrable even fatal depths, continue in her reflections as she tells of how she could have sat and sat and 'dreamt of the underground workings, the obscure passages – to be concealed for ever from human eye'. Her reflections, urged on by a visible power nothing she has ever seen can equal, turn to 'duration and decay – eternity, and perpetual wasting – the visible and *in*visible power of God and nature . . . ' The echo from her brother's mountain vision in Book VI of *The Prelude* is hardly accidental. His journey was constantly in her mind as she literally worked over the territory he had crossed as a young man and transformed into some of his great poetic passages. The apocalyptic power that Wordsworth sought for his own poetry found a true correlative in a dangerous, natural sublime.

In Dorothy's reflections the poise in nature that mingles creative and destructive forces, abides with her.[10] It is not lifted out and cast into relief by an imagination that transforms it into a mythic activity, a monumental inscription: 'workings of one mind, the features/Of the same face, blossoms upon one tree,/Characters of the great Apocalypse.' (*Prel*.VI:570) Remaining at the edge of metaphor, Dorothy was able to deploy her unique gift of description, its staying power rarely to be equalled in the writers who followed her. One could not for instance imagine a parallel reflection in her younger contemporary Mary Shelley. Danger in Mary Shelley's reflections is instantly internalised, the fragile seams of subjectivity torn open, excitations from the external world working into the turbulence incipient in the psyche, producing symbols overloaded with meaning, bearing the excess that spills over into the quest for origins.

Confronting Chaos (**Mary Shelley's** *Last Man*)

In *The Last Man* Mary Shelley fuses her notion of power, both natural and maternal, with an anxious, visionary imagination. The future closes in on consciousness. Time effectively collapses. Writing, as it arcs into time to come, is rendered impossible. The only way the novel can be imagined into existence, is backwards, by being discovered in a 'Sybilline cave', a version of the dark, contorted underworld into which Wollstonecraft, in her unfinished *Cave of Fancy* led her spirit Sagesta. The cave itself, in a kind of imaginative extremity is both the womb of Mother Nature and the tomb of all mothers. The subject of *The Last Man* is a plague that feeds on human life and can only die when mankind is annihilated. There is a single survivor, Lionel Verney, narrator of the novel. Verney however is no Frankenstein.

While Frankenstein dreamt of a new species created out of dead matter, fit to defy death, Verney grapples with the end of everything he has known or loved, with war, plague and an earth turned into a charnel house. Again and again in the novel, the human will is forced to submit to pain and humiliation. The plague overcomes the ambition of warriors just as it infects the paradise on earth, a post-Wordsworthian pastoral that Verney, who began as a primitive child of nature in the rough hill country of Cumberland, inhabits with Lord Adrian. Adrian a gentle visionary, overinformed by soul, is a clear cameo image of the dead Percy.

In this novel, Romantic longings culminate in terror. A monstrous death springs out of nature. The revolutionary impulses of Europe had failed, her beloved Shelley was dead. The author pitched her quarrel with embodiment to the end point, annihilating all possible consciousness, and mutilating that mainstay of the Romantic imagination: maternal nature.

For both William Wordsworth and Percy Shelley, there were times when the poetic imagination needed to draw on, even usurp the powers of maternal nature. For Mary Shelley the maternal image drew her whole being into a tormenting ambivalence. In *Mathilda* she had played out her version of the Proserpine myth, the daughter swallowed up by the Plutonic god, but struggling still for life. Death, which Mathilda longs for could both obliterate self-consciousness and fuse self with mother. In *The Last Man* the womb of nature permits the plague to emerge and the instabilities of human time are swallowed up in the permanence of loss. Consciousness is immensely vulnerable. Imaginative power can only come from a myth of repetition. Verney is solitary 'like our first parents expelled from Paradise'. (*LM*.234) The earth, in an inversion of the Wordsworthian figure, lies all behind him. Mother Nature is unbearably cruel:

Nature was the same, as when she was the kind mother of the human race; now, childless and forlorn, her fertility was a mockery; her loveliness a mask for deformity. Why should the breeze gently stir the trees, man felt not its refreshment? Why did dark night adorn herself with stars – man saw them not? (*LM*.239)

Mary Shelley's journal is filled with entries on reading and rereading her mother's *Letters from Sweden*. Wollstonecraft's often tender work stands in contrast to the dark negativities of her daughter's vision. Where the mother had placed maternity, both human and natural, at the very source of imaginative power, the daughter, ravaged by loss, destroys the cycles of creation and procreation.

Three chapters before the end of her novel, she cites one of the most moving of Wollstonecraft's topographical observations, embedding her mother's knowledge of origins and original power in a daughter's vision of consequences and ends. A tiny crew of survivors is struggling into the Alps leaving a plague stricken England behind them. They follow the Arve back to its source. The Mer de Glace is not mentioned. Instead comes a textual reference from the maternal source, an allusion to origins forever crossed out:

> The verdant sod, the flowery dell, and shrubbery hill were exchanged for the sky-piercing, untrodden, seedless rock, "the bones of the world, waiting to be clothed with every thing necessary to give life and beauty." Strange that we should seek shelter here! (*LM*.308)

But, of course, it is not strange. When decay has eaten up the civilised world, and unnatural death in all its melodramatic ferocity is rampant, where should one seek purity but in the rude, spare materials of creation? Testing out her mother's knowledge, the daughter finds it lacking. It is as if Maria's lost child were speaking back to her. The circumstances of life have changed irreparably, and the two lives once jointed at the source, have diverged for ever.

In her fifth letter Wollstonecraft had written of the 'frontiers' of the sea, approaching which 'nature resumed an aspect ruder and ruder, or rather seemed the bones of the world waiting to be clothed with every thing necessary to give life and beauty.' (L.42) Then followed a single sentence: 'Still it was sublime.'

Her mother's sense of grandeur is repressed in Mary Shelley's text in favour of a somewhat disjointed, somewhat forced reflection on the harshness of maternal nature: 'Surely, if, in those countries where the earth was wont, like a tender mother, to nourish her children, we had found her a destroyer, we need not seek it here, where stricken by penury she seems to shudder through her stony veins.' (LM.308-9) But having faced the facts of a shrunken origin, the voice finds that Romantic nature can still console: 'Sublime grandeur of outward objects soothed our hapless hearts and were in harmony with our desolation.' (LM.309) Perhaps this sense of sublimity could only be reached on this frozen maternal sea, as the voyagers observe a final rite, burial of 'the human form' (LM.310) By casting off their 'Mortal Birth', the plague, death's surrogate, can be overcome.

Feminine now, implicitly identified with the destruction incipient in nature, the plague gives over her powers to a last perceiving consciousness. She 'abdicated her throne, and despoiled herself of her imperial sceptre among the ice rocks that surrounded us. She left solitude and silence co-heirs of her kingdom.' (LM.310) Might one say, that using death as an imaginary instrument, and a male character as a mouthpiece, a daughter has overcome her mother? Or is that too crude a summary for what was undoubtedly one of the most complex, most fraught daughter-mother relationships in English literary history? One could rephrase the lines of argument, the better to respond by suggesting that if the mother set the script, the daughter, using her arts of subterfuge pitched to extremity, shifted the scene. To Coleridge, death had once seemed a 'strange, strange, strange Scene-shifter.' His words, both a reflection on the untimely death of his little son Berkeley and on Wordsworth's 'Slumber did my Spirit Seal', which Coleridge had assumed was inspired by Dorothy, seem particularly apt in this somewhat later context.

At the height of the plague, Verney who has gone to London, stumbles into Drury Lane Theatre. A production of *Macbeth* is in full swing. The audience is rapt, 'the first actor of the age' (presumably Edmund Kean) is ready 'to exert his powers to drug with irreflection the auditors'. (*LM*.203) With art turned into a veritable opium for the people, true reality of poverty, wretchedness and death by the plague is masked over. The scenery attempts verisimilitude to a fault. The illusion is so perfect that imagination is set free 'to revel, without fear of contradiction, or reproof from reason or the heart.' Verney describes the 'shudder like the swift passing of an electric shock' that runs through the theatre in response to Rosse's impassioned speech: 'Alas, poor country;/Almost afraid to know itself! It cannot/Be called our mother, but our grave . . . ' (*LM*.204)

In a novel sometimes marked by passages of unmitigated dreariness, the theatre episode stands out in its brilliance. Verney notes how the actor, ordinarily not of superior ability, finds his skills immeasurably sharpened by the agony of truth. He sensed 'the dangerous ground he trod'. Terrified that the audience, in an outburst of grief will overwhelm the fragile illusion, he proceeds slowly, – 'each word was drawn out with difficulty; real anguish painted his features . . . ' – as he tells Macduff of the murder of his innocent family. The audience hangs on the actor's changing expressions. What follows is perhaps not unexpected, but in its sudden rupture of boundaries between real and imaginary, is shocking nonetheless. The passage that follows in its play upon embedded quotation and represented reality, is Mary Shelley at her finest. The way in which she draws out the everpresent theme of maternity, is subtle and lively, rising above the forced rhetoric of many of her other passages:

. . . at length while Macduff, who, attending to his part, was unobservant of the highwrought sympathy of the house, cried with well acted passion:

> All my pretty ones?
> Did you say all? – O hell kite! All?
> What! All my pretty chickens, and their dam,
> At one fell swoop!

A pang of tameless grief wrenched every heart, a burst of despair was echoed from every lip. – I had entered into the universal feeling – I had been absorbed by the terrors of Rosse – I re-echoed the cry of Macduff, and then rushed out as from an hell of torture, to find calm in the free air and silent street.

Free the air was not, or the street silent. Oh, how I longed then for the dear soothings of maternal Nature . . . (*LM*.204)

The evocation of 'maternal nature' is surely relevant. In the personal mythology established by William Wordsworth, maternal nature does indeed comfort and soothe. Not only that, she conveniently gives way to the expanding powers of genius. Wordsworthian pedagogy, as Mary Jacobus has pointed out, depends on the fact of maternal death.[11] A power like nature's enters and fills the void which a mother's death creates.

The Romantic model of a void left by maternal death, which nature alone could fill, was never far from the surface of Mary Shelley's authorial consciousness. Yet its use was typically self-destructive. In *The Last Man* Lionel Verney having just witnessed the 'Golden City' of Constantinople blown up in a ball of fire, meditates on the disparity between 'blank reality' and the 'sublime fictions' of the human imagination. (*LM*.145) The scope of pedagogy in such a universe is desperately limited. There are few prior instances to draw on, and few survivors to whom knowledge, however bitterly gained from experience, can be passed on.

His bodily reserves depleted by exhaustion and hunger, Verney collapses: 'as a building whose props are loosened, and whose foundations rock, totters and falls, so when enthusiasm and hope deserted me, did my strength fail.' Truth, literal and symbolic, cohere in a grand scene of fragmentation as he sits, like Adolphe, for an instant 'on the sole remaining step of an edifice, which even in its downfall, was huge and magnificent . . .' (*LM*.146) Verney sits in a place of ruins. Nor does nature rush in to fill the void of lost affections. The building of the self does not stand alone. Wordsworthian knowledge cannot be sustained in a world where maternal nature, slowly but surely, self-destructs.

*   *   *

In his *Marriage of Heaven and Hell* William Blake set out the blueprints for a poetic method that could liberate the psyche, and create an 'improvement of sensual enjoyment'. The old Cartesian separation of mind and body had to be 'expunged'. The poet would print 'in the infernal method, by corrosives, which in Hell are salutary and medicinal, melting apparent surfaces away, and displaying the infinite which was hid.' (*B*.38) For Blake, this necessary use of 'corrosives' was underwritten by a firm belief in the indivisibility of mind and body, and the dialectical nature of progressive knowledge.

Mary Shelley was of a generation that witnessed the failure of revolutionary belief. She was Wollstonecraft's daughter, but she did not have a living mother to learn from. Her mother had died to give her birth. Mary Shelley's feminine awareness that mind could not be cleft from body drove her to an art of despair, a strategy of severe negativity. Unlike Mary Wollstonecraft, who drew back from the excesses of the Romantic sublime, Mary Shelley's version of sublimity was based on fiery consumption, the body of nature sucking back the remains of a 'wretched, engrossing self'. (*LM*.102) The phrase belongs to Perdita who had depended on the 'divinity' of sexual love to transform the 'earth common mother'. Perdita's own aspirations were absorbed in contemplation of what seemed to her a higher male excellence: 'only your power, your excellence', she wrote to Raymond, still seeking redemption through a man who has effectively abandoned her. (*LM*.101) By binding in her vision of the grand whole of life, in a jealous, sexual love, she finds herself irreparably betrayed.

But femininity betrayed can, as we have seen, take to itself, dark, colossal powers: spelling out all that subterfuge and mimicked weakness had packed away in the recesses of self. And Mary Shelley the author, picking up where Perdita stops, unleashes the forces of an imagined plague, drawing back into the womb of earth the ruined remnants of human imaginings. Just fragments of writing persist, to be discovered in a dark, prophetic cave, ground of an unimaginable beginning. She writes in large, what Dorothy Wordsworth wrote in small, at the conclusion of 'Floating Island': 'Yet the lost fragments shall remain/To fertilise some other ground.' It was a fragile hope, one that reads well from this distance in time.

Notes

Notes to Introduction: Mapping a Female Romanticism

1. Jean-Jacques Rousseau, *Émile*, transl. Barbara Foxley, (London: J.M. Dent, 1982) p. 332. Hereafter cited as *E*.

2. Mary Wollstonecraft, *Collected Letters* (ed.) Ralph Wardle (Ithaca and London: Cornell University Press, 1979) p. 141. Hereafter cited as *WL*.

3. Sandra M. Gilbert and Susan Gubar, *The Madwoman in the Attic: The Woman Writer and the Nineteenth-Century Imagination* (New Haven: Yale University Press, 1979) p. 51.

4. William Wordsworth, *The Prelude, 1799, 1805, 1850*, (eds) Jonathan Wordsworth, M.H. Abrams, Stephen Gill (New York: Norton, 1979) 6: 305-14. All references are to the 1805 *Prelude*. Hereafter cited as *Prel.* followed by book and line numbers.

5. Anne K. Mellor, *English Romantic Irony* (Cambridge: Harvard University Press, 1980) p. 5.

6. Virginia Woolf, *A Room of One's Own*, (New York: Harcourt Brace Jovanovich, 1957) p. 50.

7. This fond hope was never to be fulfilled. In October 1816, Fanny Imlay killed herself. Her sister Mary, just nineteen at the time, had given birth to two children. The first a daughter, survived only a few days. Mary had already begun work on *Frankenstein*.

8. Mary Wollstonecraft, *Letters written during a Short Residence in Sweden, Norway, and Denmark* (1796) (ed.) with an introduction by Carol H. Poston (Lincoln and London: University of Nebraska Press, 1976) p. 71. Hereafter cited as *L*.

9. For a thoughtful analysis of the pressure placed on nineteenth-century women writers by a cultural model where maternal death stands as the precondition for language and creativity, see Margaret Homans, 'Representation, Reproduction, and Women's Place in Language', *Bearing The Word, Language and Female Experience in Nineteenth-Century Women's Writing* (University of Chicago Press, 1986).

10. Percy Bysshe Shelley, *Shelley's Poetry and Prose* (eds.) Donald Reiman and Sharon Powers (New York: Norton, 1977) p. 71. Hereafter cited as *S*. followed by a page number. The phrase, which occurs in *Alastor*

echoes Wordsworth's celebrated lines in 'The Intimations Ode': 'obstinate questionings/Of sense and outward things.'

11. Mary Wollstonecraft, *A Vindication of the Rights of Woman* (1792), (ed.) Miriam Kramnick (Harmondsworth: Penguin, 1982) pp. 89,267. Hereafter cited as *V*.

12. I am indebted to Mary Poovey's study of propriety and female creativity, in Wollstonecraft and Mary Shelley. Mary Poovey, *The Proper Lady and the Woman Writer, Ideology as Style in the Works of Mary Wollstonecraft, Mary Shelley and Jane Austen* (University of Chicago Press, 1984).

13. Mary Shelley, *Mary Shelley's Journal* (ed.) F.L. Jones (Norman: University of Oklahoma Press, 1947) pp. 204,206. Hereafter cited as *MSJ*.

14. The 1831 Preface can be found in Mary Shelley, *Frankenstein, or The Modern Prometheus* (1818), (ed.) M.K. Joseph (New York: Oxford University Press, 1983) p. 5. Hereafter cited as *F*.

15. Mary Shelley, *Proserpine and Midas* (ed.) A. Koszul (London: Humphrey Milford, 1922) p. 26. Hereafter cited as *P*.

16. Mary Shelley, *The Last Man* (1826), (ed.) Hugh J. Luke (Lincoln: University of Nebraska Press, 1965) p. 80. Hereafter cited as *LM*.

17. Mary Wollstonecraft, *Mary and The Wrongs of Woman* (ed.) Gary Kelly (London: Oxford University Press, 1983) p. 75. This edition, hereafter cited as *MWW*. contains both *Mary, A Fiction* (1788) and *Maria, Or The Wrongs of Woman* (1798).

18. Thomas De Quincey, *Recollections of the Lakes and the Lake Poets* (ed.) David Wright (Harmondsworth: Penguin, 1980) p. 205. Hereafter cited as *R*.

19. Ruth Benedict, *Writings of Ruth Benedict, An Anthropologist at Work* (ed.) Margaret Mead (New York: Atherton Press, 1966) p. 519. Mead suggests that the visit to London must have occurred in 1910-11 when Benedict was twenty-two.

Notes to Chapter 1: Romantic Feminine

1. William Blake, *Poetry and Prose* (ed.) David V. Erdman, Commentary by Harold Bloom (New York: Doubleday, 1970) p. 634. Hereafter cited as *B*.

2. Theodor Adorno, *Minima Moralia, Reflections from Damaged Life*, transl. E.F.N. Jephcott (London: Verso Editions, 1985) p. 95. Hereafter cited as *A*.

3. David Aers, 'Blake: Sex, Society and Ideology', *Romanticism and Ideology, Studies in English Writing, 1765-1830* (eds) D. Aers, J. Cook,

D. Punter (London: Routledge and Kegan Paul, 1981) p. 37. See also Anne K. Mellor, 'Blake's Portrayal of Women', *Blake, An Illustrated Quarterly* (Winter 1982-3) pp. 148-155; Susan Fox, 'The Female as Metaphor in William Blake's Poetry', *Critical Inquiry* 3 (1977): 507-519; Irene Taylor, 'The Woman Scaly' *Bulletin of the Midwest Modern Language Association*, 6 (1973) pp. 74-87.

4. Friedrich von Schlegel, *Dialogue on Poetry and Literary Aphorisms* (1797-1800), transl. E. Behler, R. Struc (University Park: Pennsylvania State University Press, 1968) p. 81.

5. Mme de Staël, *De L'Allemagne*, 3 vols. (Paris: H. Nicolle, 1818) 1:255 (my translation).

6. Samuel Taylor Coleridge, *Biographia Literaria* (eds) James Engell and Walter Jackson Bate (Princeton University Press, 1984) p. 304. Hereafter cited as *BL*.

7. G.W.F. Hegel, *The Philosophy of Fine Art*, transl. F.P.B. Osmaston, 4 vols. (New York: Hacker Art Books, 1975) 1:109.

8. For an analysis of the Romantic image, though without direct reference to the feminine see Paul de Man, 'Intentional Structure of the Romantic Image,' in *Romanticism and Consciousness* (ed.) Harold Bloom (New York: Norton, 1970) p. 70; also Tilottama Rajan, *Dark Interpreter*, the Discourse of Romanticism (Ithaca: Cornell University Press, 1980) p. 23.

9. Mario Praz, *The Romantic Agony*, transl. Angus Davidson (London: Oxford University Press, 1970) p. 31.

10. See Michael Cooke, *Acts of Inclusion, Studies Bearing on an Elementary Theory of Romanticism* (New Haven: Yale University Press, 1979) p. 120.

11. John Keats, *Letters, 1814-1821*, 2 vols. (ed.) H.E. Rollins (Cambridge: Harvard University Press, 1958) 1:386-7. Hereafter cited as *K*.

12. Margaret Homans in 'Eliot, Wordsworth, and the Scenes of the Sisters' Instruction', *Critical Inquiry* 8 (1981) pp. 223-241, brings together 'Nutting' and 'Tintern Abbey' as two poems in which the sister must listen and learn.

13. William Wordsworth, *Home at Grasmere* (ed.) Beth Darlington (Ithaca: Cornell University Press, 1977) p. 45. Hereafter cited as *HG*.

14. For an extended analysis of the uses of bodily space in the Romantic self-image, see Meena Alexander, *The Poetic Self: Towards a Phenomenology of Romanticism* (New Delhi: Arnold-Heinemann, 1979).

15. Edmund Burke, *A Philosophical Enquiry into the Origin of our Ideas of the Sublime and Beautiful*, edited with an introduction by James T. Boulton (University of Notre Dame Press, 1968) p. 64. Hereafter cited as *SB*.

16. Percy Bysshe Shelley, *Shelley's Poetry and Prose* (eds) Donald Reiman and Sharon B. Powers (New York: Norton, 1977) p. 74. Hereafter cited as *S*.

Notes to Chapter 2: True Appearances

1. See Jane Roland Martin, *Reclaiming a Conversation, The Ideal of the Educated Woman* (New Haven: Yale University Press, 1985) p. 7.

2. John Gregory, *A Father's Legacy to His Daughters* (London and Edinburgh: Strahan Cadell and Creech, 1788) p. 106. Hereafter cited as *FL*.

3. Mary Wollstonecraft, *Thoughts on the Education of Daughters: with Reflections on Female Conduct in the More Important Duties of Life* (1787), (Clifton: Augustus Kelley, 1972) p. 34. Hereafter cited as *T*.

4. Quoted by Ralph M. Wardle, *Mary Wollstonecraft: A Critical Biography* (Lawrence: University of Kansas Press, 1951) p. 136.

5. Jean-Paul Sartre, *Being and Nothingness, A Phenomenological Essay on Ontology*, transl. Hazel Barnes, (New York: Pocket Books, 1966) p. 350.

6. I borrow the phrase from Judith Fetterly who argues at length that the 'first act of the feminist critic must be to become a resisting rather than an assenting reader' subjecting what is read to fierce scrutiny. Wollstonecraft, if one is to use Fetterly's phrase, stands as one of the earliest of such Romantic readers. Judith Fetterly, *The Resisting Reader: A Feminist Approach to American Fiction* (Bloomington: Indiana University Press, 1978), p. xxii.

7. William Godwin, *Memoirs of Mary Wollstonecraft* (London, 1798). This edition with preface by John Middleton Murray (New York: Richard R. Smith, 1930) p. 51. Hereafter cited as *Mem*.

8. Mary Wollstonecraft, *A Vindication of the Rights of Men, in a Letter to the Right Honourable Edmund Burke Occasioned by His Reflections on the Revolution in France* (London: Joseph Johnson, 1790) p. 9. Hereafter cited as *VRM*.

9. Edmund Burke, *Reflections on the Revolution in France* (1790) (New York: Anchor Press, 1973), p. 89. Yet it is by no means clear that Wollstonecraft herself was free of the faults she saw so prominently displayed in Burke.

10. See Florence Boos, 'Catherine Macaulay's Letters on Education: An Early Feminist Polemic,' *University of Michigan Papers in Women's Studies* 2.2 (1976) pp. 64-78. Boos points out that Letters XXI-XXIV are the most striking sources for Wollstonecraft's *A Vindication of the Rights of Woman* p. 71.

11. Catherine Macaulay, *Letters on Education with Observations on Religious*

and Metaphysical Subjects (1790), (New York: Garland Publishing, 1974) p. 214. Hereafter cited as *LE*.

12. Wollstonecraft's review of Mme D'Arblay's (Fanny Burney) *Camilla: Or A Picture of Youth* in *Analytical Review* 24 (1796) p. 148.

13. Michel Foucault, *Madness and Civilization, A History of Insanity in the Age of Reason,* transl. Richard Howard (New York: Vintage, 1971) pp. 85-6.

14. See Gayatri Chakravorty Spivak, 'Sex and History in *The Prelude* (1805): Books Nine to Thirteen', *Texas Studies in Language and Literature* 23.3 (1981) pp. 324-59.

15. Claire Tomalin sets out the details of what is known of the friendship between Wollstonecraft and Mme Roland. *The Life and Death of Mary Wollstonecraft* (New York: Harcourt Brace Jovanovich, 1983) pp. 134-8.

16. Janet Todd, *Women's Friendship in Literature* (New York: Columbia University Press, 1980) pp. 208-26.

17. 'Sigismonda and Guiscardo, from Boccace', *The Poems and Fables of John Dryden* (ed). James Kinsley (London: Oxford University Press, 1962) p. 631.

Notes to Chapter 3: Of Mothers and Mamas

1. For further reference see Rachel Mayer Brownstein, 'The Private Life: Dorothy Wordsworth's Journals', *Modern Language Quarterly* 34 (1973) pp. 48-63.

2. Letter of April 1794 to Jane Pollard, *The Letters of William and Dorothy Wordsworth: The Early Years, 1787-1805* (eds) Ernest de Selincourt, Chester Shaver (London: Clarendon Press, 1967) p. 111. Hereafter cited as *EY*.

3. The way in which the activity of walking underpins the textuality of the journals is developed in Meena Alexander, 'Dorothy Wordsworth: The Grounds of Writing', *Women's Studies*, vol.14 (1987) no.3, pp. 195-210.

4. Julia Kristeva *Revolution in Poetic Language*, transl. Margaret Waller (New York: Columbia University Press, 1984) p. 26.

5. *Dorothy Wordsworth's Commonplace Book*, Dove Cottage Manuscript 26, 145v. Hereafter cited as *DC.MS.26*.

6. Letter to Coleridge in 1802, *Letters of Charles and Mary Lamb, 1796-1802* (ed.) E.V. Lucas, 3 vols. (New Haven: Yale University Press, 1935) 3. 326.

7. See Heather Glen, *Vision and Disenchantment: Blake's Songs and Wordsworth's Lyrical Ballads* (Cambridge University Press, 1983).

8. Mary Wollstonecraft, *Original Stories from Real Life; with Conversations. Calculated to Regulate the Affections and Form the Mind to Truth and Goodness*

(1788), (London: Joseph Johnson, 1791). Hereafter cited as *OS*. Followed by a page number.

9. See Dennis Welch, 'Blake's Response to Wollstonecraft's *Original Stories*', *Blake: An Illustrated Quarterly* 13 (Summer 1979) 1, pp. 4-15.

10. Still what strikes a modern reader as cruelty might have seemed nothing other than a necessary realism to a reader of Wollstonecraft's time. Mrs Trimmer for instance in her *Easy Introduction to the Knowledge of Nature* (Philadelphia: Carey and Son, 1821) p. 23 can tell of young Henry who warned not to eat green fruit, disobeys his mother only to suffer a dreadful death from the 'live worms' that infect his bowels.

11. Simone de Beauvoir, *The Second Sex*, transl. H.M. Parshley (New York: Vintage, 1974) p. 480.

12. Adrienne Rich, 'Conditions for Work: The Common World of Women' in *Working it Out* (eds) Sara Ruddick and Pamela Daniels (New York: Pantheon, 1977) p. xvi.

13. Nel Noddings, *Caring, A Feminine Approach to Ethical and Moral Education* (Berkeley: University of California Press, 1984) pp. 41,44.

14. *The Journals of Dorothy Wordsworth: The Alfoxden Journal (1798), The Grasmere Journals (1800-3) (ed.)* Mary Moorman (Oxford University Press, 1971) p. 67. Hereafter cited as *AGJ*.

15. Sara Ruddick, 'Maternal Thinking' in *Mothering, Essays in Feminist Theory* (ed.) Joyce Trebilcot (Totowa: Rowan and Allanheld, 1984) pp. 213-30.

16. 'Mary Jones and her Pet Lamb,' Dove Cottage Manuscript 121 (6r-6v). Hereafter cited as *DC.MS.121*.

17. Susan Levin, *Dorothy Wordsworth and Romanticism* (New Brunswick: Rutgers University Press, 1987) p. 45. In her Appendices, Levin includes an edition of 'Mary Jones and her Pet Lamb'.

18. Adrienne Rich, *The Dream of a Common Language, Poems 1974-1977* (New York: Norton, 1978) p. 3.

19. Thomas De Quincey, *Recollections of the Lakes and the Lake Poets* (ed.) David Wright (Harmondsworth: Penguin, 1970) p. 188. Hereafter cited as *R*.

20. William Wordsworth, *Poetical Works*, 5 vols. (eds) E. de Selincourt, H. Darbishire (London: Clarendon Press, 1940-9) 2:216. Hereafter cited as *PW*.

21. Jacques Lacan, *Ecrits, A Selection*, transl. Alan Sheridan (New York: Norton, 1977) p. 104.

22. Marlon Ross elaborates on this point: 'Naturalizing Gender: Woman's Place in Wordsworth's Ideological Landscape', *English Literary History* 53 (1986), pp. 391-410. Wordsworth's poetic strategy squares with Sherry

Ortner's argument that in every culture woman is defined 'as being of a lower order of existence than itself'. Sherry Ortner, 'Is Female to Male as Nature is to Culture?' *Women, Culture and Society*, (eds) Michelle Rosaldo and Louise Lamphere (Stanford University Press, 1974).

Notes to Chapter 4: Writing in Fragments

1. Dorothy Wordsworth, *Recollections of a Tour Made in Scotland* (1803) in *Journals of Dorothy Wordsworth*, 2 vols. (ed.) Ernest de Selincourt, vol. I (London: Macmillan, 1952) p. 207 (hereafter cited as *JDW*. followed by volume and page numbers.

2. Elizabeth Hardwick in *Seduction and Betrayal, Women and Literature* (New York: Vintage, 1975) p. 149.

3. I borrow the phrase from de Selincourt, *Dorothy Wordsworth: A Biography* (Oxford: Clarendon Press, 1933) p. 393.

4. *The Letters of William and Dorothy Wordsworth: The Later Years, 1821-1850* (ed.) Ernest de Selincourt, revised Alan G. Hill (London: Clarendon Press, 1976-82). Hereafter cited as *LY*. Both the letters I have quoted are in Part 3, pp. 528,598. Hereafter cited as *LY*.

5. The poem is inscribed in Dorothy Wordsworth's later *Commonplace Book*, Dove Cottage Manuscript 120, $55^v - 53^v$ (The manuscript will hereafter be cited as *DC. MS. 120*). It is reprinted in Susan Levin (1987).

6. In *Women Writers and Poetic Identity* (Princeton University Press, 1980) p. 41. Margaret Homans argues that gender was a powerful inhibiting force on Dorothy's possible growth as a poet.

7. *The Letters of William and Dorothy Wordsworth, Middle Years, 1806-1811* (eds) Ernest de Selincourt, Mary Moorman (London: Clarendon Press, 1969) p. 25. Hereafter cited as *MY*.

8. Ruskin characterises the 'Pathetic Fallacy' as the result of intense feelings which falsify the nature of the object perceived. He distinguishes 'the ordinary, proper and true appearances of things to us from our own emotional projections, the extraordinary or false appearances, when we are under the influence of emotion or contemplative fancy'. John Ruskin, *Modern Painters*, 5 vols. (Kent: George Allen, 1888) 3: 159. Chapter XII: 'Of the Pathetic Fallacy'.

9. S.T. Coleridge, *The Collected Letters of Samuel Taylor Coleridge* (ed.) E.L. Griggs vol.1, 1785-1800 (Oxford: Clarendon Press, 1956) pp. 330-31. Hereafter cited as *CL*.

10. Edward Young, *The Complaint; or, Night Thoughts on Life, Death and Immortality*, Night VI, 414-16, in *The Works of the Author of the Night Thoughts*, revised and corrected by himself, 3 vols. (London: Dodsley, Dilly, Cadell et.al., MDCCXCII) 2: 327.

Notes to Chapter 5: Natural Enclosures

1. Virginia Woolf, *The Second Common Reader* (New York: Harcourt Brace Jovanovich, 1960) p. 149. Hereafter cited as *SCR*.

2. *Mrs Dalloway* (New York: Harcourt Brace Jovanovich, 1953) p. 45.

3. Jonathan Wordsworth, *William Wordsworth, The Borders of Vision* (Oxford: Clarendon Press, 1982) p. 129. David Hartley writes of how just as our imperfect languages improve and purify, so human life might 'gradually tend to a collection of pure pleasures only'. *Observations on Man* (ed.) H. Pistorius, 3 vols. (London: Johnson, 1791) I. pp. 320-1.

4. Letter of Annette Vallon to William Wordsworth (20 March, 1793) included in Appendix II of Emile Legouis, *William Wordsworth and Annette Vallon* (London: Dent and Sons, 1922) p. 125.

5. Dorothy Wordsworth, Commonplace Book, Dove Cottage Manuscript 120. (Hereafter cited as *DC.MS.120*.) Though no dates are given, the poem is copied immediately after 'Lines intended for Edith Southey's Album, Composed in June 1832 in recollection of a request made by her some years ago, and of my own promise till now unfulfilled'. *DC.MS.120* is paginated 1-89 and written in from both sides. The 'Floating Island' runs from 61^r – 60^v. It is immediately followed by the poem 'Thoughts on my sick-bed'.

6. *DC.MS.26*. This earlier Commonplace Book which contains the entry 'John's Language' opens with the lines: 'William Wordsworth, Grasmere, Jan 27, 1800'. The entry on Aristotle is entitled 'From Aristotle's Synopsis of the Virtues and Vices'. (45r) It comes from *The Nichomachean Ethics*, Book 3, Chapter 6 where Aristotle reflects on courage.

7. William Wordsworth, *Guide to the Lakes* (ed.) Ernest de Selincourt (Oxford University Press, 1982) p. 38.

8. *DC.MS.26*, 41^r–42^v. The extracts are from John Barrow, *Travels in China* (London: Cadell and Davies, 1804) Dorothy must have read the book shortly after it appeared. Barrow writes of 'Shing Moo': '*The character* Shing is compounded of *ear*, *mouth*, and *ruler*, or *king*, intending perhaps *the faculty of knowing all that ear has heard and mouth uttered.*' (p. 472)

9. *DC.MS.120* (72^v–71^v)

10. Gaston Bachelard, *The Poetics of Space*, transl. Maria Jolas (Boston: Beacon Press, 1969) p. 17.

11. Samuel Taylor Coleridge, *Biographia Literaria* (ed.) with his *Aesthetical Essays*, J. Shawcross, 2 vols. (London: Oxford University Press, 1907) 2:257. Later in the same essay Coleridge clarifies his point arguing that the artist ought to imitate 'that which is within the thing, that which is active through form and figure . . . the *Natur-geist*, or spirit of nature'. (2:259)

12. *DC.MS.120* (71^r–70^v), 'A Winter's Ramble in Grasmere Vale',

consists of ten stanzas. The first seven stanzas also form part of a separate poem, 'Grasmere, A Fragment' which includes as its earlier portion the stanzas of 'A Cottage in Grasmere Vale'. The two stanzas of the brief 'After Recollection at sight of the same cottage' hook together the two larger chunks of 'Grasmere, A Fragment'. William Knight's edition of *The Poetical Works of William Wordsworth* (London: Macmillan, 1896), 8:259-262. Knight prints it from the 1805 MS where it was included as an appendix to Dorothy's *Recollections of a Tour in Scotland*.

13. Barbara Schapiro, *The Romantic Mother: Narcissistic Patterns in Romantic Poetry* (Baltimore: Johns Hopkins University Press, 1983), p. 94.

14. Homans, *Women Writers and Poetic Identity*, p. 81.

15. Charlotte Brontë, *Villette*, edited by Mark Lilly, Introduction by Tony Tanner (Harmondsworth: Penguin, 1979) p. 112.

16. Dorothy Wordsworth, *George and Sarah Green, a Narrative*, edited and with a Preface by Ernest de Selincourt (Oxford: Clarendon Press, 1936) p. 41. Hereafter cited as *GSG*.

17. The lines occur in 'Irregular Stanzas – Holiday at Gwendovennant – May 1826' *DC.MS.120* (73^v).

18. The phrase is found in 'Lines intended for My Niece's Album' *DC.MS.120* (64^v).

19. Dove Cottage Manuscript 64, *George and Sarah Green*.

Notes to Chapter 6: Unnatural Creation

1. Ellen Moers, *Literary Women* (New York: Doubleday, 1977) p. 142.

2. Robert Kiely, *The Romantic Novel in England* (Cambridge: Harvard University Press, 1972) p. 164.

3. William Veeder in *Mary Shelley and Frankenstein, The Fate of Androgyny* (University of Chicago Press, 1986) makes an intricate study of Mary Shelley's sometimes tormented bond with the ideal of androgyny: as she discovered it in Percy's work and as it emerged in her own life and art.

4. Adorno, *Minima Moralia*, p. 95.

5. Dorothy Dinnerstein, *The Mermaid and the Minotaur, Sexual Arrangements and Human Malaise* (New York: Harper and Row, 1976) p. 155.

6. Harold Bloom, *The Anxiety of Influence* (New York: Oxford University Press, 1973).

7. Anne Mellor, *Mary Shelley: Her Life, Her Fiction, Her Monsters* (London: Methuen, 1988) pp. 172,176.

8. Wolfgang Kayser, *The Grotesque in Literature and Art*, transl. Ulrich Weisstein (Bloomington: Indiana University Press, 1963) p. 185.

9. Mary Shelley, *Collected Tales and Stories* (ed.) Charles E. Robinson (Baltimore: Johns Hopkins University Press, 1976) p. 128. Hereafter cited as *CT*.

Notes to Chapter 7: Revising the Feminine

1. Jean-Paul Sartre, 'Une Idée fondamentale de la phenomenologie de Husserl,' *Situations*: 1 (Paris: Gallimard, 1947) pp. 31-2 (my translation).

2. F.W. Bateson, *Wordsworth: A Reinterpretation* (London: Longmans, Green and Company, 1954) p. 153; cf. Geoffrey Durrant, *William Wordsworth* (London: Cambridge University Press, 1969); Richard E. Matlak, 'Wordsworth's Lucy Poems in Psychobiographical Context,' *PMLA*, 93 (1978) pp. 46-65.

3. Richard Fadem elaborates on the feminine image in 'Tintern Abbey' and Dorothy's late readings of herself in that poem: 'Dorothy Wordsworth: A View from "Tintern Abbey"', *Wordsworth Circle*, IX (Winter 1978) 1, pp. 17-32.

4. Letter from the Duke of Argyle to the Rev. T.S. Howson, September 1848. Portion of it is quoted in the Notes to de Selincourt's edition of Wordsworth's poetry, *PW* 2:517.

5. Letter of June 1837 to Catherine Clarkson in *The Letters of Mary Wordsworth, 1800-1855* (ed.) Mary E. Burton (Oxford: Clarendon Press, 1958) p. 157.

6. Mary Shelley, *Mathilda* (ed. Elizabeth Nitchie), *Studies in Philology*, Extra Series no. 3. (Chapel Hill: University of North Carolina Press, 1959) p. 1. Hereafter cited as *M*.

7. Mary Shelley, *The Letters of Mary Wollstonecraft Shelley*, 2 vols. (ed.) Betty T. Bennett (Baltimore: Johns Hopkins University Press, 1980) I, p. 376. Hereafter cited as *MSL*.

Notes to Chapter 8: Versions of the Sublime

1. M.H. Abrams, *Natural Supernaturalism, Tradition and Revelation in Romantic Literature* (New York: Norton, 1973) p. 27.

2. Thomas Weiskel, *The Romantic Sublime, Studies in the Structure and Psychology of Transcendence* (Baltimore: Johns Hopkins Press, 1976) p. 4.

3. Sampson Reed, *Observations on the Growth of the Mind* (Boston, 1826), cited in Perry Miller, *The Transcendentalists* (Cambridge: Harvard University Press, 1950) p. 58.

4. Hester Chapone, *Letters on the Improvement of the Mind* (1773)

in *The Works of Hester Chapone*, 4 vols. (Boston: Wells and Wait, 1809) 4:147.

5. Jean-Jacques Rousseau, *The Reveries of the Solitary Walker* transl. Charles Butterworth (New York: Harper and Row, 1979) p. 12. Hereafter cited as *SW*, followed by a page number.

6. The concept of the *époche* or the 'phenomenological reduction' was first outlined by Edmund Husserl in *The Idea of Phenomenology* (1907) and developed in *Ideas* (1913). In its initial form – in order to clarify the structures of consciousness – it calls for a total suspension of belief in the status of the external world: 'Every thesis related to this objectivity', wrote Husserl, 'must be disconnected . . . ' Edmund Husserl, *Ideas, General Introduction to Pure Phenomenology*, transl. W.R. Boyce-Gibson (London: Allen and Unwin, 1952) p. 110.

7. Simone Weil, *Waiting for God*, transl. Emma Crauford (New York: G.P. Putnam's, 1951) pp. 115,159.

8. Thomas McFarland, *Romanticism and the Forms of Ruin: Wordsworth, Coleridge and the Modalities of Fragmentation* (Princeton University Press, 1981) p. 28.

9. Marc A. Rubenstein, ' "My Accursed Origin": The Search for the Mother in *Frankenstein*', *Studies in Romanticism*, 15 (Spring 1976) 2, p. 174.

10. Homans in *Bearing the Word* suggests that Dorothy, often in complex and involuted ways, consistently literalises her brother's symbols, a function of her own feminine imagination.

11. Mary Jacobus, ' "Behold the Parent Hen": Pedagogy and *The Prelude*', Paper delivered at the English Institute, Harvard University, August, 1986.

Selected Bibliography

Mary Wollstonecraft (1759-97)

Thoughts on the Education of Daughters: with Reflections on Female Conduct in the More Important Duties of Life (1787), (Clifton: Augustus Kelley, 1972).

Original Stories from Real Life; with Conversations. Calculated to Regulate the Affections and Form the Mind to Truth and Goodness (1788), (London: Joseph Johnson, 1791).

Mary and The Wrongs of Woman (ed.) Gary Kelly (London: Oxford University Press, 1983); this edition contains *Mary, A Fiction* (1788) and *Maria or The Wrongs of Woman* (1798).

A Vindication of the Rights of Men, in a Letter to the Right Honourable Edmund Burke Occasioned by His Reflections on the Revolution in France (1790), (London: Joseph Johnson, 1790).

A Vindication of the Rights of Woman with Strictures on Political and Moral Subjects (1792) (ed.) Miriam Kramnick (Harmondsworth: Penguin, 1982).

Letters written during a Short Residence in Sweden, Norway, and Denmark, (1796), (ed.) Carol H. Poston (Lincoln and London: University of Nebraska Press, 1976).

Posthumous Works of the Author of A Vindication of the Rights of Woman, (ed.) William Godwin (1798), (Clifton: Augustus Kelley, 1972).

Collected Letters (ed.) Ralph Wardle (Ithaca and London: Cornell University Press, 1979).

Dorothy Wordsworth (1771-1855)

The Journals of Dorothy Wordsworth: The Alfoxden Journal (1798), The Grasmere Journals (1800-3), (ed.) Mary Moorman (Oxford University Press, 1971).

Journals of Dorothy Wordsworth, 2 vols. (ed.) Ernest de Selincourt (London: Macmillan, 1952).

George and Sarah Green, a Narrative (ed.) Ernest de Selincourt (Oxford: Clarendon Press, 1936).

George and Sarah Green, Dove Cottage Manuscript 64.

'Mary Jones and her Pet Lamb', Dove Cottage Manuscript 121.

Commonplace Book, Dove Cottage Manuscript 120.

Commonplace Book, Dove Cottage Manuscript 26.

The Letters of William and Dorothy Wordsworth (eds) Alan Hill, Mary Moorman, Chester Shaver (Oxford: Clarendon Press, 1967-82).

Mary Shelley (1797-1851)

Frankenstein, or the Modern Prometheus, (1818), (ed.) M.K. Joseph (New York: Oxford University Press, 1983).

Mathilda, (1819), (ed.) Elizabeth Nitchie, *Studies in Philology*, Extra Series no. 3. (Chapel Hill: University of North Carolina Press, 1959).

Proserpine and Midas (ed.) A. Koszul (London: Humphrey Milford, 1922) (*Proserpine* (1820), publ. 1832).

The Last Man (1826), (ed.) Hugh J. Luke (Lincoln: University of Nebraska Press, 1965).

Collected Tales and Stories (ed.) Charles E. Robinson (Baltimore: Johns Hopkins University Press, 1976).

Mary Shelley's Journal (ed.) F.L. Jones (Norman: University of Oklahoma Press, 1947).

The Journals of Mary Shelley 1814-1844 (ed.) Paula

R. Feldman and Diana Scott-Kilvert (Oxford: The Clarendon Press, 1987) 2 vols.

The Letters of Mary Wollstonecraft Shelley, 3 vols. (ed.) Betty T. Bennett (Baltimore: Johns Hopkins University Press, 1980, 1983, 1988).

Selected Bibliography II

M.H. Abrams, *Natural Supernaturalism, Tradition and Revelation in Romantic Literature* (New York: Norton, 1973).

D. Aers, J. Cook, D. Punter (eds) *Romanticism and Ideology, Studies in English Writing, 1765-1830* (London: Routledge and Kegan Paul, 1981).

Meena Alexander, *The Poetic Self, Towards a Phenomenology of Romanticism* (Atlantic Highlands: Humanities Press, 1981).

Meena Alexander, 'Wordsworth: The Sea and its Double', *Analecta Husserliana: The Yearbook of Phenomenological Research* Vol.XIX (Dordecht: Reidel, 1985) pp. 77-84.

Meena Alexander, 'Dorothy Wordsworth: The Grounds of Writing', *Women's Studies*, 14 (1987) 3, pp. 195-210.

Gaston Bachelard, *The Poetics of Space*, transl. Maria Jolas (Boston: Beacon Press, 1969).

William Blake, *Poetry and Prose* (ed.) David V. Erdman, Commentary by Harold Bloom (New York: Doubleday, 1970).

Edmund Burke, *A Philosophical Enquiry into the Origin of our Ideas of the Sublime and Beautiful*, edited with an introduction by James T. Boulton (University of Notre Dame Press, 1968).

Michael Cooke, *Acts of Inclusion, Studies Bearing on an Elementary Theory of Romanticism* (New Haven: Yale University Press, 1979).

Dorothy Dinnerstein, *The Mermaid and the Minotaur*,

Sexual Arrangements and Human Malaise (New York: Harper and Row, 1976).

Judith Fetterly, *The Resisting Reader: A Feminist Approach to American Fiction* (Bloomington: Indiana University Press, 1978).

Michel Foucault, *Madness and Civilization, A History of Insanity in the Age of Reason*, transl. Richard Howard (New York: Vintage, 1971).

Sandra M. Gilbert and Susan Gubar, *The Madwoman in the Attic: The Woman Writer and the Nineteenth-Century Imagination* (New Haven: Yale University Press, 1979).

Carol Gilligan, *In a Different Voice, Psychological Theory and Women's Development* (Cambridge: Harvard University Press, 1982).

William Godwin, *Memoirs of Mary Wollstonecraft* (1798), (New York: Richard R. Smith, 1930).

Dr John Gregory, *A Father's Legacy to His Daughters* (London and Edinburgh: Strahan Cadell and Creech, 1788).

Elizabeth Hardwick, *Seduction and Betrayal, Women and Literature* (New York: Vintage, 1975).

Margaret Homans, *Women Writers and Poetic Identity* (Princeton University Press, 1980).

Margaret Homans, *Bearing The Word, Language and Female Experience in Nineteenth-Century Women's Writing* (University of Chicago Press, 1986).

Mary Jacobus (ed.) *Women Writing and Writing about Women* (New York: Barnes and Noble, 1979).

Mary Jacobus, *Reading Woman, Essays in Feminist Criticism* (New York: Columbia University Press, 1986)

Mary Jacobus, ' "Behold the Parent Hen": Pedagogy and *The Prelude*', Paper delivered at the English Institute, Harvard University, August, 1986.

Wolfgang Kayser, *The Grotesque in Literature and Art*, transl. Ulrich Weisstein (Bloomington: Indiana University Press, 1963).

Robert Kiely, *The Romantic Novel in England* (Cambridge: Harvard University Press, 1972).

Julia Kristeva, *Revolution in Poetic Language*, transl. Margaret Waller (New York: Columbia University Press, 1984).

Jacques Lacan, *Ecrits, A Selection*, transl. Alan Sheridan (New York: Norton, 1977).

Jacques Lacan, *The Four Fundamental Concepts of Psycho-Analysis*, transl. Alan Sheridan (ed.) Jacques-Alain Miller (New York: Norton, 1978).

Susan Levin, *Dorothy Wordsworth and Romanticism* (New Brunswick: Rutgers University Press, 1987).

Catherine Macaulay, *Letters on Education with Observations on Religious and Metaphysical Subjects* (1790), (New York: Garland Publishing, 1974).

Paul de Man, 'Intentional Structure of the Romantic Image,' in *Romanticism and Consciousness* (ed.) Harold Bloom (New York: Norton, 1970).

Jane Roland Martin, *Reclaiming a Conversation, The Ideal of the Educated Woman* (New Haven: Yale University Press, 1985).

Thomas McFarland, *Romanticism and the Forms of Ruin: Wordsworth, Coleridge and the Modalities of Fragmentation* (Princeton University Press, 1981).

Jerome McGann, *The Romantic Ideology, A Critical Investigation* (University of Chicago Press, 1983).

Anne K. Mellor, *English Romantic Irony* (Cambridge: Harvard University Press, 1980).

Anne K. Mellor, *Mary Shelley: Her Life, Her Fiction, Her Monsters* (London: Methuen, 1988).

Anne K. Mellor (ed.) *Romanticism and Feminism* (Bloomington: Indiana University Press, 1988).

Maurice Merleau-Ponty, *Phenomenology of Perception*, transl. C. Smith (London: Routledge and Kegan Paul, 1962).

Ellen Moers, *Literary Women* (New York: Doubleday, 1977).

Nel Noddings, *Caring, A Feminine Approach to Ethical and Moral Education* (Berkley: University of California Press, 1984).

Sherry Ortner, 'Is Female to Male as Nature is to Culture?' *Women, Culture and Society* (eds) Michelle Rosaldo and Louise Lamphere (Stanford: Stanford University Press, 1974).

Mary Poovey, *The Proper Lady and the Woman Writer, Ideology as Style in the Works of Mary Wollstonecraft, Mary Shelley and Jane Austen* (University of Chicago Press, 1984).

Mario Praz, *The Romantic Agony* transl. Angus Davidson (London: Oxford University Press, 1970).

Thomas De Quincey, *Recollections of the Lakes and the Lake Poets* (ed.) David Wright (Harmondsworth: Penguin, 1980).

Tilottama Rajan, *Dark Interpreter, the Discourse of Romanticism* (Ithaca: Cornell University Press, 1980).

Adrienne Rich, 'Conditions for Work: The Common World of Women' in *Working it Out* (eds.) Sara Ruddick and Pamela Daniels (New York: Pantheon, 1977).

Adrienne Rich, *The Dream of a Common Language, Poems 1974-1977* (New York: Norton, 1978).

Marlon Ross, 'Naturalizing Gender: Woman's Place in Wordsworth's Ideological Landscape,' *ELH* 53 (1986) pp. 391-410.

Jean-Jacques Rousseau, *Émile*, transl. Barbara Foxley, introduction by P.D. Jimack (London: J.M. Dent, 1982).

Jean-Jacques Rousseau, *The Reveries of the Solitary Walker*, transl. Charles Butterworth (New York: Harper and Row, 1979).

Marc A. Rubenstein, ' "My Accursed Origin": The Search for the Mother in *Frankenstein*', *Studies in Romanticism*, 15 (Spring, 1976) 2.

Sara Ruddick, 'Maternal Thinking' *Mothering, Essays in*

Feminist Theory (ed.) Joyce Trebilcot (Totowa: Rowan and Allanheld, 1984) pp. 213-30.

Barbara Schapiro, *The Romantic Mother: Narcissistic Patterns in Romantic Poetry* (Baltimore: Johns Hopkins University Press, 1983).

F.W. Schlegel, *Dialogue on Poetry and Literary Aphorisms* (1797-1800) transl. E. Behler, R. Struc (University Park: Pennsylvania State University Press, 1968).

Ernest de Selincourt, *Dorothy Wordsworth: A Biography* (Oxford: Clarendon Press, 1933).

Percy Bysshe Shelley, *Shelley's Poetry and Prose* (eds) Donald Reiman and Sharon B. Powers (New York: Norton, 1977).

The Letters of Percy Bysshe Shelley, 2 vols. (ed.) Frederick L. Jones (Oxford: Clarendon Press, 1964).

Elaine Showalter, *A Literature of Their Own: British Women Novelists from Brontë to Lessing* (Princeton University Press, 1977).

Mme de Staël, *De L'Allemagne*, 3 vols. (Paris: H. Nicolle, 1818).

Lee Sterrenburg, '*The Last Man*: Anatomy of Failed Revolutions'. *Nineteenth-Century Fiction*, 33 (1978). pp. 324-47.

Janet Todd, *Women's Friendship in Literature* (New York: Columbia University Press, 1980).

Claire Tomalin, *The Life and Death of Mary Wollstonecraft* (New York: Harcourt Brace Jovanovich, 1983).

William Veeder, *Mary Shelley and Frankenstein, The Fate of Androgyny* (University of Chicago Press, 1986).

Ralph M. Wardle, *Mary Wollstonecraft: A Critical Biography* (Lawrence: University of Kansas Press, 1951).

Thomas Weiskel, *The Romantic Sublime, Studies in the Structure and Psychology of Transcendence* (Baltimore: Johns Hopkins Press, 1976).

Virginia Woolf, *A Room of One's Own*, (New York: Harcourt Brace Jovanovich, 1957).

Virginia Woolf, *The Second Common Reader* (New York: Harcourt Brace Jovanovich, 1960).

Jonathan Wordsworth, *William Wordsworth, The Borders of Vision* (Oxford: Clarendon Press, 1982).

Mary Wordsworth, *The Letters of Mary Wordsworth, 1800-1855* (ed.) Mary E. Burton (Oxford: Clarendon Press, 1958).

William Wordsworth, *The Prelude, 1799, 1805, 1850* (eds) Jonathan Wordsworth, M.H. Abrams, Stephen Gill (New York: Norton, 1979).

William Wordsworth, *Home at Grasmere* (ed.) Beth Darlington (Ithaca: Cornell University Press, 1977).

William Wordsworth, *Poetical Works*, 5 vols. (eds) E. de Selincourt, H. Darbishire (London: Clarendon Press, 1940-9).

Index